WOMAN'S JOURNEY TO WHOLENESS

A book about woman's search for self and a deeper
meaning in her life through spiritual awakening.

Teresa,
Dare to
pursue your
inner search wealth
you have a wealth
of knowledge within'
Love,
Hara

WOMAN'S JOURNEY TO WHOLENESS

A book about woman's search for self and a deeper meaning in her life through spiritual awakening.

Hara Glen

Ruteldge Books, Inc.

Danbury, CT

Rutledge Books, Inc.
107 Mill Plain Road, Danbury, CT 06811
1-800-278-8533
www.rutledgebooks.com

Manufactured in the United States of America

Cataloging in Publication Data
Glen, Hara
Woman's Journey to Wholeness: A book about woman's search for self and a deeper meaning in her life through spiritual awakening.

ISBN: 1-58244-196-0

1. Woman's issues. 2. Spiritual. 3. Inner nature of woman.
4. Self-esteem and self-fulfillment.

Library of Congress Control Number: 2001093828

Contents

Dedication

This book is dedicated to my loving sister, Carol, who has always been supportive of me during my times of difficult change and my times of great joy. Thank you from the bottom of my heart. I also want to thank my husband, my children, and grandchildren for their encouragement and enthusiasm overseeing this book come to life.

About the Author

Hara Glen is a teacher, counselor, business woman, mentor, wife, mother and grandmother. She is dedicated to discovering wholeness within herself physically, mentally, emotionally, and spiritually. Her spiritual studies go back some forty years. In *Woman's Journey to Wholeness* she describes her personal passage to renewal and healing that has allowed her to find deeper meaning in her life. Her eloquent and compassionate style will touch you deeply and provide for you a way to access that inner part of yourself that calls out for self-expression and a sense of well being.

In her book she shares some of her fascinating experiences. Her incredible story about learning she had breast cancer and how she dealt with it will give women hope and courage to act in a new way with their own illnesses. Hara transformed her experience by letting go of fear and allowing the healing power of the Divine take her through this challenge.

This is Hara's first book, but definitely not her first in

writing about psychological and spiritual ideas. Her intuitive abilities have helped her see life in a new perspective. Her compassionate way of taking you on her own spiritual voyage to healing will warm your heart and instill in you ideas of how to move through many of life's challenges.

The conversational style used in this book evokes the voice of a favorite teacher or mentor. Women will connect with the messages as they desperately seek to find themselves in today's hectic society with its many demands.

Preface

This is the time for "woman" to be all she is meant to be. As you read this book, listen to what your heart is telling you because it knows what you yearn for, and it knows how to change what is not working in your life. I have struggled through many challenges in my lifetime, and it wasn't until I learned to take my "quiet times" seriously that I was able to touch my inner source of love, creativity, and wisdom. We are so much more than we think we are.

We often struggle with what we feel in our hearts to be right for us. Courage is needed as we heed the call and take our first step toward the birth of a new idea or a dream tucked away in our hearts. As I took my first step at writing this book I felt both feelings of excitement and fear. But, in my heart I knew something wonderful was to be born. I had to stretch the creative parameters of my mind, as well as touch the very essence of who I am.

I hope some of the messages in this book will open doors for you to see beyond your present vision of yourself. "Woman" has only touched the outer layer of her potential. The changes you are willing to make now can bring so much joy, fulfillment, and healing to you. You do not have to do it alone. When you are ready to change, help comes in many forms. I encourage each of you to lift yourself up a little further so you can get a new perspective on who you are and what life is calling you to do.

IT'S ALL A JOURNEY . . .

Hara

For More Information: http://www.expage.com/haraglen

CHAPTER ONE

WOMAN'S SEARCH FOR SELF

There is a great deal of talk today about the role of women in our society. I believe this is an extremely important time for us because many of us will be asked to go beyond our present identities and desires and to search out the very depth of our being. What we need to know will come to us in different ways, but if we are willing to change, we will receive the wisdom to make the proper choices in our lives.

There are more opportunities for women in the workplace, so we can pretty much choose a job that will be right for our growth at this time. Relationships are being tested because at the deeper spiritual level of us we are finally seeing how powerful, intelligent, deserving, loving, and intuitive we are. And, more than ever, we are identifying with the inner core of ourselves. Now, it is our job to respect and honor this in ourselves. By doing so, we will not only change our lives as women, but will ultimately help to bridge the gap between conflicting relationships with our partners.

There are some basic skills we need to learn in communicating our feelings and our innermost desires. We are going a step up from the level of support groups and private therapy, not that these should be totally abandoned. I am talking about a personal inner journey where we connect with our higher power. This results in a relationship so deep and so revealing that we will not always be able to adequately express what is happening. However, we will intuitively know we are on the right pathway.

I tell you this from experience. I *know* the feelings of assurance and guidance I get from my Divine source, and I confess it has taken me a long time to understand the value of taking time to *ask* for the guidance, not to mention the willingness to wait for the answers. I continue to dedicate myself to this practice because making a wise choice from the beginning saves so much time, effort and, often, heartache.

As humans, we try to control everything ourselves, and when we become desperate we go to our higher power. Let us learn to ask for divine guidance before our choices are made. Know that this is an act of loving yourself. Many, many women have been in some kind of therapy or twelve-step program. These women realize the importance of going deeper within themselves for the answers. They have learned to face life through better understanding of themselves, learning to love themselves at a deeper level, and by sharing their stories with other women.

Women who have had life-threatening diseases know what I am talking about for they have had to shed so much of their earlier beliefs and create new life patterns for themselves in order to survive and, more than that, to really LIVE! But, let's not wait until a crisis awakens us. There's a universal energy moving that indicates it is time to look at our lives right now and create something much better for ourselves. It requires a stripping away of that which is destructive or just is not valid any longer, and it takes a willingness to really love ourselves by getting to know who we are at the very depth of our being. This is the "search" I am referring to. In order to find peace within ourselves, we must find out more of who we are.

So, who are you? What do you really know about yourself? What role do you see yourself in? Do you want to stay there? Most of us have at least learned enough Shakespeare to recall these lines from *Hamlet*: *"This above all, to thine own self be true."* But, we must find the "self" before we can be true to it. The search for self has always been and always will be. It is possible that you will uncover a good deal of the authentic self by having quiet time and allowing something within you to come forth and declare what your gift to yourself and to humanity is.

When you are ready to accept this unexplored part of you, help will come. You may find it by reading spiritual works, some of you will want counseling, some will find it in church, others in twelve-step programs, and some will be transformed through a crisis. It is important to know that help is available, and it will come in a variety of ways depending on your dedication to grow and change.

Some of you may not be ready for real soul-searching, but I know an awful lot of women know their lives need changing and intuitively they know it is of a spiritual nature. We women know when there is something unsettling in our lives. Some of us can face it; others cannot, and those who cannot often take the path of addiction so they don't have to deal with the emotional pain.

Many women are quite satisfied in their early years of marriage. And, during times of childbearing and domestic responsibilities it sometimes seems enough. But, more and more women are searching for their identities beyond home-maker, wife, mother, caretaker, and guardian of the hearts and spirits of those they love. This does not have to mean we shirk our duties. It is simply part of the evolving of "woman." But, we must take caution that we find a balance in where our energies go.

We must honor our basic role of feminine nurturing. If we have not found a fulfilling outlet for our inner callings, we must do so because that is an important part of who we are. Some women find this early in their lives. My daughter knew she wanted to be a teacher when she was ten years old and that is what she did. Others find it somewhere along life's pathway. If we don't, in the years that follow raising a family, many women will feel lost and the dreams will fade. But, we only need to go within to recapture our earlier yearnings. It may not be exactly as we pictured it long ago, but it can be something absolutely perfect for us now.

I urge the young women in their twenties and thirties to see the years ahead as a time for infinite possibilities. If you begin your inner journey now, you will be able to limit the number of crisis you fall into because you have made wise choices along life's pathway. I realize these early years are when you are devoted to careers and, perhaps, marriage. That happens to be the reason why spiritual awakening is so valuable.

The inner journey you will have taken will keep you from panicking as you approach your later years. You will not feel that life is passing you by when you get in your forties and fifties. Life does not pass us by. *We stop the creative process* because of our fears and our dissatisfaction with life. These years are meant to focus more on who you are, and it can be a very exciting time of your life. At forty the intuition is begging to be sharpened, and if you take the time to go within to seek out new ways of viewing your participation in life, you will be astonished at what comes up.

We must rid ourselves of the stigma that we start going downhill at forty or fifty. The more you are willing to go within and listen, the more you will realize there is so much more to you than you could possibly imagine. You may spend time looking for a few gray hairs and slight signs of a wrinkle, but doing that only magnifies the fear you already have inside of you. Let life guide you in this part of your journey. Stay open to new experiences. You can transform your life by getting in touch with the "authentic self" which allows you to see the beliefs that have held you back from feeling good about yourself. Remember, there's part of you that you haven't yet discovered.

Changing our perception of life is not a simple thing to do because we have been living by the rules of our society, and many times these rules pull us away from WHO WE ARE. Giving birth to our new "authentic self" can be like giving birth to a child. If we are holding on to the fear of change and fighting the pain, the birth is often delayed. But, the process has begun, and we have the opportunity to bring forth the creative seed planted, thus transforming our lives.

As painful as it sometimes feels, a natural rhythm is available to us for reaching the ultimate goal, but we must trust something greater than ourselves to help us breathe through the transition and do the work that is necessary to prepare for the new birth. In childbirth, holding the child makes the pain worthwhile. And so it is with birthing parts of ourselves that have been masked due to fear, blaming others, and not being quite ready to accept the spiritual help that is beckoning us to come out and be who we are.

It takes a lot of faith to keep moving forward. There will be moments when you begin to doubt. But, I urge you to stay with the process because, when you do, you accept your precious gift. You are finally able to catch a glimpse of your own magnificence. Because you always have free choice, you can refrain from giving birth to the event. That is the easy way, but you lose so much. Sometimes you get another chance, and sometimes you don't.

Stay alert to what life is telling you, and be willing to answer the call. I remember the feelings I had when I was forty-five years old and starting up a business of my own. I had a tremendous urge to do this. I felt confident that I had the knowledge to do it, but my mind was filled with fearful thoughts. I was single and relied on just my own means of supporting myself other than a small amount of settlement from my first marriage. I desperately wanted to take on this challenge because I understood how these opportunities come along at just the right times, and it's important to grasp onto them immediately even with our knees shaking and heart pounding. The power of choice is incredibly important here, and it usually calls for us to stretch beyond what we thought was possible. I got a name for my new business, selected stationery, got checks printed, and tended to all the various other details.

One day as I was out purchasing some of the necessary items to begin my business, I panicked. I pulled my car over to the curb and sobbed my heart out. When I got myself together again, I comforted myself. I knew I must let go of the fear and continue to ask for Divine guidance. By reminding myself that a power much greater than myself was forever guiding this whole venture, I was able to let the fear go. So many things opened up for me that it was apparent I had made the right choice. It is okay to feel the fear, but keep up your inner dialogue with that part of you that is all-knowing, all-loving, and all-powerful.

My business was successful in spite of some who warned me it was a great risk. There are times to tune out to well-meaning friends. When I made my decision to go with this new venture, it was what my heart told me and not what my intellect said. I did not make a huge amount of money, but be aware of thinking that success means only the amount of money you make. What I gained in self-worth, self-fulfill-ment, and business experience was far more valuable than money. It was a big lesson for me to learn to trust my own inner wisdom. Don't let these precious times go by without a dedicated search within, sticking with what you believe to be right, and moving forward. I know each one of you has talents and desires that need expressing. Dare to tap into them for they are eager to express themselves.

More women than ever before are dedicated to being all they are meant to be. We do not always make choices that seem right for us, but I believe we can use all experiences to help us create something better for ourselves as we continue our jour-ney through life. It is important to take each step in the journey and know it is only for that time. There is always more, but be grateful for what you have now!

Women, by nature, are intuitive. If we will be still long enough, we will get the messages to help us make constructive changes in our lives. So many of us want to control everything ourselves, to use our intellect as our main guide, but I believe we will never, ever find out who we are until we tap that inner place where the creative process begins. There are losses and gains in life, to be sure. The only sense of permanence and stability has to come from within us. There is a greater plan for us that we often cannot see, and we will not feel the happiness and joy that is our natural inheritance until we change according to this greater plan.

We often work so hard to achieve something, and yet it should be natural because we are relying on a greater source of wisdom and energy to direct us. We have the choice of asking for guidance and waiting for it, believing it will come, or to control every means to get it now. That guidance may come in various guises, but it will come. We will be given the strength and wisdom to choose what is right for us at any given time if we only ask.

When we begin to see more clearly who we are. . . the deeper self that has a sense of peace and well-being. . . we will come closer to our "authentic self." We will know when this begins to take place because we will feel comfortable and at home with ourselves. And, we will treat ourselves with reverence and respect.

Writing is a wonderful way to connect with ourselves at a deeper level. We can get a clearer picture of who we are and what we believe in if we will tap into our own feeling nature. Keep the thought that you are special and that you are here to give of your love and your natural talents. During your "quiet time," write down the ideas and feelings that come to you. At first it will take discipline to do this, but keep it simple.

When we speak of "discipline" we often think it is something very hard to do. I once read that discipline means choices. Every time you say "yes" to a goal or objective, you say "no" to many more. The prize is the YES and the price is the NO. Never confuse discipline with rigidity. Certainly, perfection is not the aim; rather, strive for the peace of mind that comes from being in charge of yourself. True discipline achieves a balance of producing, but not pushing; of diligence, not driving. Disciplined people are happier people because they are fulfilling inner potential.

We often sabotage ourselves by trying to make writing a big project. It is okay if you don't write anything on certain days, but keep a notebook and pen near by. And, notice how you feel once you have made some notes. Read them over and over again so you can feel the accomplishment of making some breakthrough in what you are feeling and what you are believing about yourself, and about your life.

I am fortunate that writing is easy for me. I have drawers of paper describing my feelings at particularly difficult times, and it has helped me to heal many hurts by seeing a clearer picture of how I was living my life. When I wrote my autobiography I realized there were still areas of my life that needed healing. I found parts of myself that had been hidden. When I would begin to write about my parents who were deceased or about a certain challenging event, the tears would come, and I knew there was even more to heal.

Sometimes it was heart wrenching, but after the pain came an immense sense of release. And, sometimes I would cry about the *happy* events of the past. Writing was a way in which I externalized my feelings. Believe me, we are prone to hold on to our pain as though it belonged to us. Sometimes we are so much into our own emotional pain that we forget the joyful experiences we have had along the way. Give yourself permission to release that which holds you back from your good.

I have also come to believe that our emotional and our physical pain often serve a need, and it is important to look at this and see what that need might be. Certainly, we can learn to get our needs met without carrying negative feelings around or being sick. I once heard a woman who was badly crippled with arthritis say, "I'd rather die than let my husband know he is right." We really have to look at whether or not we are trying to control someone else at our own expense. You may have backaches a lot so you have periods of time you must stay in bed and rest. Backaches on a regular basis means you do not feel supported or you are doing more than your body can handle. Or, your challenge may be in learning to speak up for yourself, knowing you can get your needs met in a healthy way instead of pushing the anger down and letting it fester, feeling hopeless about changing anything. The result is you end up with some kind of an "attention-getter" illness.

If we are serious about living honestly and passionately, we must look beyond the symptoms so we can get to the source of the problem. There is nothing so terrible in our lives that cannot be healed. It is only a question of whether or not we are willing to go through the feelings, accept ourselves unconditionally, and forgive others as well as ourselves. And, a nice dose of inspiration helps. This process changes us dramatically. There is a transcendence in mind, body, and spirit. This is important to understand. Writing is not essential to reach this state, but it is extremely helpful.

I, personally, learned that through my writing I was able to get in touch with thoughts and feelings that were somewhere inside of me needing to surface. Because of my deeper understanding of the danger of suppressing my feelings, I came to accept my own sensitive nature so much more. For many years I had thought something was wrong with me because I felt so deeply, and it was almost impossible for me to keep my feelings inside. They had to come out. Today, I am grateful that I have the capacity to feel and to acknowledge those feelings, and to know this process contributes greatly to my self-worth and my total well-being.

What is difficult to accept in your own life? Your height? Your weight? Shyness? A physical handicap? A challenging relationship? When you come to terms with the thing you don't like about yourself, you will find yourself opening up to something new and exciting. You will begin to see how talented and special you are. There is so much you need to learn about yourself. When you once begin to explore more about who you are, it will amaze you at what comes up.

Through the years all of us have taken on certain roles and values either from family or society, and we believe this is who we really are. But, many of these beliefs may no longer be appropriate for us as adults. Some of us are operating on old agendas of which we are often not even aware. Some of those roles might be "The Scapegoat", "The Lost Child", "The Caretaker", "The Rebel", "The Hero", or "The Perfect Child." These roles were not chosen. They served a purpose in the day-to-day functioning of a troubled family system. However, when men and women continue to play out these roles in their adult years, the true self continues to be buried.

While growing up, I was the "caretaker", especially where the emotions were concerned. I tried to make it better for, not only members of my family, but others as well. In that role, I lost some of my sense of self. This is not always a traumatic thing, as many children find their role satisfying, and it works for them in their adult years. However, there are many who live troubled lives because the events of a difficult early family life have etched the scars very deep and their lives have been adversely affected.

My own feeling was, "Why do I react in such a negative way when I carry my 'caretaker' role too far?" The answer is, because my energy becomes depleted, and I find myself exhausted and resentful. If you are interested in understanding more regarding childhood roles in dysfunctional families, get John Bradshaw's book, *Bradshaw on: The Family*. All of this role playing significantly contributes to who you think you are, your ability to function in a healthy way, and your contribution to society, as a whole.

Knowing that our beliefs significantly affect WHO WE ARE, we must first become conscious of what we believe; to articulate it and to see whether or not these beliefs are in harmony with who we think we are: our values, our goals, our relationships. I find it extremely beneficial to continue to look at my own beliefs and to see whether or not I am in my "caretaker" role to the extent where it shadows the real me. In some ways I can see the conflict of dual roles in my life, so I ask myself this question: "Are my beliefs congruent with who I say I am, or do I say one thing and live another?"

Look at your relationships with men. What is your experience telling you? Look at how you treat yourself as a woman. Where does that belief come from, and do you want to change it? Do you feel abundance in your financial affairs or are you always in debt? Do you believe in lack and limitation or do you believe in abundance? Is your God a loving God, or do you stay in a state of fear wondering whether or not you are doomed for punishment? Living out our experiences does not rely on luck or happenstance. We create our world according to our beliefs, so we'd better know what is lurking in the back of our minds.

Fear is something that is often learned early, and our society at present seems to perpetuate this emotion by trying to instill fear in us at every turn in the road. You will hear it every day on television, read it every day in the newspapers and magazines, and far too many movies are fear based. There are many people who constantly live in fear. They are so used to thinking negatively that they don't realize the base of their thinking is fear. If you are in a state of fear a lot of the time, really look at this because fear will interfere with you becoming all you are meant to be. Fear snuffs out your dreams and your aspirations. If you continually feel your world is not a safe place to be, you will stay stuck in fear.

Of course there are some reasons for us to take caution, but living in fear day after day truly robs us of our good. We do not need to listen to all of the fear-oriented stories from television, or read them in the newspapers. We have free choice to seek out that which reminds us of what is true for us. I certainly believe each of us needs to use some good sense about our decisions. Our world is not perfect. There are those who do not honor themselves, thus do not honor others. Face your fears head-on. Don't let fear rule your life. Going within will counteract fear. Seek that quiet place within you where you will find peace. When you do this, you will discover more of who you are, and you will live out your experiences in a way that promotes healthy choices, leaving fear behind.

As you begin to see how creative you are and how easy it is to tap that part of yourself that is all-knowing, you will be ready to give up the fear. You won't make a lot of changes at first, and maybe you won't need to. I know fear grips us all at times, keeping us from seeing things clearly. But, as we become conscious of our thoughts and feelings, moving ourselves *through* the fear, we will be better able to get ourselves back on track.

Of course, we have basic protective fears that are necessary, but I'm speaking about the ones we create in our own mind that are absolutely unfounded. Be aware of where the power is coming from. . . what was the driving force in making certain choices and putting yourself in the "fear" mode? Do you think things through? Are you going to believe what someone else says, or are you going to tap your own inner source where you will gain guidance and direction that ultimately can lead to something right and good for yourself?

A very prevalent fear is not having enough money, but many times it is ones own desire to have much more than they need. Power of money and fame alone will never bring you lasting happiness, or peace of mind. However, money could be a by-product of your new state of awareness, bringing you a sense of fulfillment and also allowing you to enjoy the things that money can buy. It is in balancing out our lives that we are able to truly enjoy the journey along the way.

Is the process of getting to know ourselves scary? It certainly can be because it requires us to be very honest with ourselves. Will you change so drastically that your partner may feel threatened? First of all, it takes quite a while to make big changes in our lives. Some men have very uneasy feelings when their partner changes her behavior, so you need to move forward with compassion for those you love. My suggestion is that you discuss with your partner what you are doing and why. Every situation is different, so you need to have some "quiet time" and go about your changes in the way that seems right for you.

If your partner is experiencing addictive behavior and not in a twelve-step program, you may get resistance, especially if he is in denial. Denial is a common resistance to change and is often associated with the feeling of shame. Therefore, it is not always easy to seek out what you want for yourself. You may feel your circumstances and the behaviors of your partner keep you from growing and changing.

One example of this is when a partner of a practicing alcoholic denies there is a problem. There is an unspoken agreement in many families that they don't talk about it. But, the feelings are there, and until help is sought out, there will be dysfunctional behavior in their lives, however subtle it may seem. Also, you may have a "just too hard to face" attitude thinking you really can't change anything, so why try? It often takes a courageous member of the family to confront the alcoholic, hopefully with the support of others in the family. I had to do that with my daughter and it was difficult. Remember, help is available through a program called Al-Anon. Any AA hotline can give you a phone number.

Many women stay in unhealthy relationships because they are afraid to go out on their own for one reason or another, or because some cultures dictate certain behavior for women which results in extremely low self-worth. The belief system of these women is "I'm not good enough to experience any better." We need to help these women find value in themselves. Changes are beginning to take place in some countries like Iran, Japan, China, and others, where the women are speaking out by demanding more rights, but the process is slow.

Being under someone else's total control for a long time

injures the very spirit of a woman. It takes gentle, loving, and understanding people to help these women recover their spirits and to see how valuable and creative they really are. When this is accomplished, they will not tolerate being mistreated nor will they stay in a relationship that does not support who they are. Fears like "What will become of me?" and extremely low self-worth keep many women from ever seeing their true potential. . . their "authentic selves." Yes, it can be a tough barrier to break through. But, as woman's worth becomes an open issue there is hope for others to follow.

If more women continue the search within, dropping the fears and false dependencies, there is a tremendous amount of hope for massive changes to take place. It will take being responsible for your own life. And, it will mean seriously looking at what is not working for you *now*. Give this plenty of time. Write down what you want to change and what approach you are going to take. Talk it over with your partner, and maybe your children. This is important because at first, your husband, children, or whomever else, will probably not like the changes you make. Often, the family dynamics have been in play for a long time and the rules have been set.

My children didn't always like some changes I made earlier in my life, but now as adults they understand. I *did* get out of my marriage to their father, and that was extremely painful for them. I knew the time was right to be on my own because there was a part of me left somewhere in the wilderness, wanting so badly to find the way. . . to seek out who I was beyond my role as wife and mother. I was fortunate to have had an understanding husband who wanted the best for me, so we parted friends. .

You may feel stuck. . . no way out. It depends on the individuals involved and the circumstances surrounding the marriage. I have found that once you make a commitment to becoming your "authentic self", that part of you will not let you go unless you totally abort your intention to change. As you continue your search, you will see that what you are really doing is setting yourself free. There is an exhilarating feeling that goes with this process, and you will feel an assurance that you are on the right path.

From former clients, and from the many people I come in contact with, I have realized how poorly we often communicate our feelings. We let things build up in us and then make a rash decision or a sudden outburst of emotions. I know of a husband who, after thirty years of marriage, left a note for his wife saying he wanted a divorce. He had moved his things out while she was away. Come to find out, they had never discussed anything about either party being dissatisfied in the marriage, so the wife was in shock followed by a great deal of anger. Recently, a woman I know told her husband to leave the house without ever discussing some of the hurts and anger she was feeling. And, there are thousands of similar stories out there.

We must stop hurting each other this way. I, too, have made some drastic changes without enough consideration for others. At that time, I didn't know how to do it differently. I do now. We need to be as gentle as possible because many times we are deeply hurting someone else, as well as ourselves. The message can be said in a way that has some compassion. I am a real advocate of communicating. Why is it we cannot sit down and share our feelings when they come up rather than stuffing them until we are out of control or totally irrational? I know it is difficult to do this if the other party is unwilling, but it is our duty to at least try.

If you haven't learned how to share your feelings, start learning now! It could save you a lot of heartache later. By sharing your feelings you become vulnerable, so slowly move toward saying what you feel in your heart. Write it out if it is difficult for you. You will soon feel safe in doing so. I suspect the safety issue is a lot of the reason why it is so difficult for us to open up and reveal what has been stored away so long and, no doubt, grown in its intensity. I know this is a challenge, so can we be open to new, healthy ways of communicating? It takes special skills to clearly state our feelings, but we can work toward learning them.

These are times of great searching for women to find their true identity. Society pulls us every which way, but if we are still long enough and consult our hearts, we will begin to catch a glimpse of who we are. It is imperative we have a lot of support during this time. Many of us have been "people pleasers," and it is understandable that our families and friends will not like it if we begin to say "no." There is a proper balance, but even then we will be told we are selfish. It is important to get through this stage because until we learn to honor ourselves, we will be in conflict with who we are. We will carry resentments and we will feel incomplete.

We must not bury our dreams and aspirations. I certainly have been through my own search, and I am pleased to say that I made it through the transition. I was fortunate to have a tremendous amount of loving support during my most crucial periods of growth, mainly from friends who were also seeking to unveil that which had been covered for so long and to let go of old beliefs that no longer served them. I have a loving family, but I came to see that help from them was minimal. They see you in your earlier roles and assuming they liked those roles, they don't want you to change. Sometimes we think we have lost the love of a child or spouse because we choose a new pathway that feels right for us. After much change, my children gave me love and acceptance, and that is a lot.

It is too much to ask our children to support us in some of our major changes, so we must seek our support elsewhere. A belief in a power greater than ourselves is an essential component of support. It doesn't matter what the religious faith or belief is, only that it must be loving and support the idea of an inner wisdom directed by a loving and Divine power where change is not only possible, but inevitable. Having the support of other human beings is also crucial.

There is a tremendous amount of help available to us in today's world. There are twelve-step programs for most addictions, and they are free. There are telephone hot lines, books, churches, therapists, mentors, and friends. The help is out there. Believe me, when we are ready to change, help comes, but we must be in a place of willingness to move forward and a willingness to let go of our fears. Be very kind to yourself as you embrace change. Seek out the support of other women. We all hold enough emotional pain, so we are great confidants.

I see such a need to come together in love and acceptance of all women knowing each of us has our story of being mistreated, misunderstood, ignored, put down, or misused in some way. And, there are many women who are in denial over what is even happening to them. It sometimes is shocking to see how many women stay in relationships that continually feed them only negative thoughts about who they are.

These women carry a lot of emotional pain and feel they just don't count.

Simply knowing there are feminine spirits sending them love and supportive energy can help to move them toward getting help for themselves. There is power in numbers, and there is power in the energy we put out to bring about change. It will be a "coming together" of woman's innate power made up of the true feminine qualities of compassion, cooperation, tolerance, intuition, and nurturance. Yes, women have masculine qualities as well such as strong, assertive, goal oriented, and the ability to focus, but basically we are feminine. This coming together doesn't always have to be on a personal level. It can be with the energy you carry in your own personal life; the choices YOU make, how YOU stand up for yourself, and how YOU treat other women that will change the overall consciousness of "woman."

Those of us who have broken through the barriers to find more about who we are can speak for all women in so many different ways; through support groups, in social situations, at work, and right in our own homes. As we begin to really accept who we are, we will be much more tolerant of those who continue to struggle toward self-worth. Those whom we have criticized in the past have merely been those who are trying to find their way. If we act with compassion, it will empower us to make incredible changes in how society views women. Yes, we have made a lot of progress, but there are still millions of women out there who cry in secret because they feel helpless and hopeless.

Chapter Two
New Beginnings

All that I have written so far may sound nice to you, but so very impossible to achieve. Let me say, changing and growing is a step-by-step process. There are no magic wands; we begin where we are, WHEREVER THAT IS. We begin to strip away the outer protection and the fear, and we move toward more understanding of who we are. We begin to touch that inner source of wisdom that helps us create new ideas and ways to bring them to fruition. If you could talk with as many women as I have and listened to their stories, you would cry. Many women are in deep conflict with who they are, and many women just don't want to let go of the blaming. Their hearts are hardened because the hurts are deep, and they find it difficult to forgive.

Yes, there are times when all seems painfully unfair but, the good news is we can change, and we can take responsibility for our own lives by making new choices. If we don't forgive, we carry a very heavy burden. The forgiving frees us to move on to the "New Beginnings." We need to do this, first for ourselves, and then to be a part of a massive movement to bring women to a place of dignity, respect, and honor.

We are nurturers of the souls that come into our lives. This is a high calling, so we must prepare ourselves through greater awareness of who we are and of the gifts we have to offer. This preparation includes nurturing all ideas concerning self-worth and self-love. There are subtle ways in which we put ourselves down, or allow someone else to put us down. As you become more aware of what you are doing, you will stop it, and when you have liberated yourself from your limited thinking, you will not allow others to act in any harmful way toward you.

Taking responsibility for yourself is the key. Your journey within will assist you in discovering ways to feel good about yourself. Many times it is the small things that are most important, such as being willing to give yourself some hugs or taking time to lovingly nurture yourself. Self love requires a commitment on your part: first, to become more aware of what your relationship is with yourself right now, and to continue the journey to wholeness by growing and changing. A part of us knows we have been chosen to make a difference, so enter that deeper part of you that can guide you. What a difference it will make as each of us begins to search out our individual talents and express them.

I made my commitment to self-growth by beginning a simple eight step program:

1 - SLOW DOWN. Inner wisdom cannot come while constantly rushing.
2 - HAVE QUIET TIME 10-15 MINUTES PER DAY. Deep breathing helps. (This is a form of meditation. Light a candle to help make it a spiritual experience.)
3 - DURING QUIET TIME, GET IN TOUCH WITH YOUR FEELINGS. TELL YOURSELF IT IS SAFE TO DO THIS.

If you have deep traumas, go for professional help.

4 - ASK FOR DIVINE GUIDANCE.

5 - WRITE WHAT YOU ARE FEELING IN A NOTEBOOK. KEEP IT SIMPLE.

6 - REMIND YOURSELF EVERY DAY THAT YOU ARE WORTH THIS TIME ALONE.

It is an act of loving yourself.

7 - IF YOU MISS A DAY, DO NOT FEEL GUILTY, AND DO NOT GIVE UP.

8 - GIVE THANKS FOR WHAT YOU HAVE NOW KNOWING MORE WILL COME TO YOU.

Using this simple guide gave me a sense of beginning to make changes without it being so overwhelming. You may find a better way to begin. This is just a suggestion. Remember, pushing yourself to get it all NOW will end in failure to move forward. Let your journey unfold in a natural way.

It's not that it is so hard to change our lives; it is our resistance to change that is the enemy. And, I believe the basis of the resistance is our lack of self-worth and our lack of faith in something greater than ourselves to help us. Some people stay with something very painful only because it is familiar to them. I know that sounds strange, but psychologists and psychiatrists through the years have seen this pattern. Remember, you have lived with certain beliefs and fears for a long time, and sometimes it seems easier to hold onto them than to change.

You will need to show a great deal of trust as you move through your "New Beginning." Try not to get discouraged. The road may seem bumpy for awhile, but if you stay with a simple plan, you will begin to feel differently inside. Just hang on. That's the best suggestion I can give you because I have gone through many challenges, and I know in my heart that my Divine source is my strength and my guide. That source may direct you to other people who will give you help and insight. For example, someone will mention a person who does a particular type of therapy, or you will notice a book on display in the bookstore that is calling out to you. We often think it is a coincidence that these people or things appear at just the right time, but it is all a part of our readiness to grow and change.

My "quiet times" have been a source of comfort, inspiration, and an opening for my creativity to flow. And best of all, I have built a trust in myself that allows me to travel the unknown because I know I can rely on Divine guidance for help. We are not meant to "go it" alone. There's a part of ourselves we'll never know if we do not spend time alone to tap our inner resources.

Let go of the resistance and open yourself to that creative process that forever lives within you. It's beckoning you to create something new. Start with just a small thing if you have a hard time with change. It could be something as simple as planting a new flower in the garden, spending more time with your family, changing your hairdo, or taking a trip to a place you've longed to see. Creating something new stretches us and shows us that we can do more than we think we can.

Because we have free choice, we can stay just the way we are, but staying the same is often difficult because life has a way of bringing unexpected changes such as someone special dying, you are let go from a job, or you go through a divorce. It's as though life is prompting us to be more, and it is time to learn that we are supported at these difficult times. This is all part of the journey.

My life has been filled with change, but I am an adventuresome person and have welcomed most of the changes. However, it is never easy to make the transition. Opening our hearts and our minds and asking for guidance is the key. Allow yourself to feel the fears within you, but hold on to your faith knowing new dynamics are coming in and you are preparing yourself for something wonderful; that new birth I spoke about earlier in the book. Stay open to receiving the gift.

The process of change is often disconcerting, but keep reminding yourself that you are guided and protected, and that it is time for something new to enter your life. Talk to yourself. It is okay to admit your fear. Stare it right in the face, and then move on. The easy way is to abort the new creation, but that will just throw you back into the old situation that you have been trying to change. In order to create something new, I have found one essential thing I must do and that is to have "quiet time" each day, if only for five or ten minutes. Giving yourself periodic moments of silence throughout the day also works.

With all of the distractions in today's society, we are often thrown off balance by too much busyness and too much stress. At those times, we need to be still. We all fall short in establishing a relationship with our inner selves. It is something that we need to daily remind ourselves of. The more we connect with the inner, the easier it gets to build on this relationship that is always there for us.

When change hits us by surprise, we often blame someone else for what is happening. It's time to rid ourselves of the blaming and realize these events can be great opportunities to go beyond what we have done in the past. It took me a lot of years to get to the place where I realized that it wasn't all those other people out there who were causing my unrest and my emotional pain. I fought this idea because I was not ready to take responsibility for my own life. And, it didn't occur to me that I had the power to change; to create something new. There's so much we can do if we stay open to change and tap our inner resources. If you believe there are people out there who keep you from your good, you are holding yourself back from finding your true purpose in life. No one else is doing this to you!

At about thirty-eight years old I took a major step in my own growth. It was one of those times when I had a deep urge to try something new in my life. My children were older; one in high school, one in junior high, and one in elementary school. So, I decided to volunteer part time at a private school for retarded children. At first, my work with the children and the parents showed me how fortunate I was to have children who were able to function normally. But, my greatest gift came in finding an outlet for my love of children and, at the same time, to realize I had a talent that I wasn't even aware of.

The speech pathologist praised me for my insights and willingness to create new ways of motivating the students to learn. After a year of volunteer work, I was asked to join the staff as a speech coordinator for the program. It was only the beginning of a number of things that I did for myself to promote greater fulfillment and greater self-worth. I was very much aware of my need to give back to life. Giving to others is an important part of our spiritual growth. I brought excitement and lots of love into every day I worked. I began to see the incredible "me." I knew the timing was perfect for me to discover more about myself, and I welcomed this change. The seven years I worked at that school brought me an immense amount of self-confidence which I desperately needed.

If you stay tuned into your inner desires and nudgings, you will feel a special energy when the time is right to make changes, and your changes will be in harmony with who you are. I learned to sense what my needs were and to work toward meeting them the best I could for that time. I learned to be very kind and gentle with myself as I worked toward creating a more fulfilling life. I talked to myself a lot, referring to myself as "honey."

My journey toward loving myself more was well on the way. I complimented myself when I was able to accomplish something new, and when I made mistakes I was gentle with myself. . . well, most of the time. To begin with, I wasn't always as loving, but over time it became natural for me to stop and talk endearingly to myself. Criticizing ourselves for not doing something well enough only sets us back, and we end up blaming ourselves for not being smart enough, fast enough, or creative enough. Can you see how loving ourselves is interwoven into all of our journey to spiritual wholeness?

If you are used to the "highs" you get on your adrenaline actions, you will go crazy sitting ten to fifteen minutes per day, just being quiet. But remind yourself that this is a "New Beginning." You will want to abandon your "quiet time" because you think it is not doing any good. This is the ego's way of wanting to have instant gratification. It does not recognize something it cannot identify by the five senses. Knowing this, you can counter this temptation by making the choice to continue your "quiet time," if only for five or ten minutes.

Sticking with this beginning program guarantees you a great start in the changes you want to make. Once you establish the habit, you won't ever want to give it up. If you are like me, you will find all kinds of reasons why you don't have time for these eight steps, or you will get into your fast pace of living and forget. Just don't get discouraged and give up. If you doubt the worth of such a beginning program, do it anyway, or create your own program, because this is the critical point at which you will really begin to benefit from it. This is the time when new energy comes in to support you. Perhaps what you have to look at is that you have just taken on too much, and you need to let go of something.

With every single step you take in becoming more aware, you will begin to see some positive changes. It is not easy; old fears, beliefs, and patterns are not easily discarded. Part of why I am writing this book is to tell women that by working through your own destructive patterns, emotional pain, and unhappiness, there will be such a burst of self-worth that you will have a sense of excitement in pursuing the necessary changes in your life. Once you get that first glimpse of what it means to really love yourself, you're on your way.

My heart tells me this is the time for women to move forward, using our combined talents and genuine concerns to assist "woman" to be all she is meant to be. This is about instilling a sense of freedom in us so we express who we are, and we need to let other women know that who we are is important. This is not the ego bragging. It is the very soul of us coming forth to claim its victory.

Over the years many brave and committed women have brought us to where we are now, and there is so much more. You can be a part of the new changes. Today, more people than you can imagine are seeking to understand more about their capacity to grow and to change. We aren't locked into a certain pathway just because our parents chose a particular lifestyle, profession, or belief. We are realizing that we are individuals with a uniqueness that needs to express itself. There is no one exactly like us.

As we grow and change, it is important that we share our stories so other women will have hope. Let your stories include what you are doing during the difficult times to bring you to a place of greater understanding and greater wonder of your capacity to be "more." It will take looking at your beliefs and changing what no longer works for you. Whatever you have learned from your parents or grandparents (and bless them) that is not in alignment with WHO YOU ARE, work on releasing these beliefs. It's incredibly important to do this because, as we grow individually, we participate in the healing of all women. By creating greater peace, love, and harmony within our own lives it becomes part of an energy system that encompasses all of us. It is important that we verbally share our beliefs with other women and be part of a support system for greater collective healing.

I still have so much to learn, but I can only share where I have been, what I have learned, what I have changed, and where I am now. And, I know there is much more! The creative process never stops. There are unlimited possibilities available to us, but we need to be in a place where we become aware of them. This is being conscious of what you are thinking and what you are doing. Check out what your thoughts are concerning change.

Sometimes you will feel fearful. Let that be okay, but move through the fear and take some form of action. Believe me, there's an exciting creative experience waiting for you. Break down your wall of resistance toward change. Some of the resistance may come from a loved one who wants everything to stay just as it is. Deal with this challenge the best you can, but move forward. I know it is not easy for a partner to see his mate make too many changes. Beware that you don't use hurtful tactics thinking this is the only way to move forward. We must act compassionately, but firmly.

We don't have to find an excuse for wanting to be who we are meant to be. We can learn to make changes that enhance our own growth and still support our partners and loved ones. No, it will not be easy, but be sure to take those few minutes to be still and go within. Check out your motivation and intention in making this change. Ask for Divine guidance in following through with it in a loving way. There are no perfect ways to do something. Each of us must search our own heart and do what we feel is best at any particular time. Trust that the greater power and intelligence is assisting you.

It is becoming clearer to me that there is a purpose for all things, and that there is a natural progression of evolving into that which the Creator has deemed right for us at any given time. We may regret some of the choices we have made in the past, but let's not stay stuck there. We cannot change the past, but we can change how we live our lives RIGHT NOW by being in tune with the energies that show us when it is appropriate to change something and when it is not.

If you create "quiet time" for yourself, you will get in touch with these creative energies. It is not something you have to work hard to accomplish. This is about just "being there" enough with your inner wisdom to receive the message when it is time to act in a new way. And, when it is time, you will receive everything you need to bring it forth. This may sound too good to be true, but I can tell you from experience, IT WORKS!

Create this "New Beginning" with a zest that you would put into a beloved hobby or project. Or, think of it as weaving a beautiful tapestry of your life, and you can put in all the things that serve your own best interest and the best interest of those you love and care for. It can be a masterpiece!

As you create your "New Beginning", it is important to get in touch with your feelings. We women have a history of stuffing our feelings so long that they manifest in very unhealthy ways. Men would often say, and maybe still do, "Oh, she's just having a bad day. She'll get over it." And we bought into it. Somewhere along the way we have been taught that it is not acceptable to express how we feel about something especially if it pertains to our emotional hurts.

Our feelings are valid, whatever they may be, and we'd better learn to express them or we will be in conflict with ourselves. And, if they are held in for a long time, the probability becomes greater they will contribute to some of our physical illnesses. We, as women, will not have emotional breakdowns if we learn to vent our feelings as they come up! Most men have a long way to go in expressing their feelings. For many generations they have been taught they should not show what they feel because it is not manly. In my opinion, we have little hope for seeing much of a difference in our relationships until this kind of belief is changed.

Our society functions in ways to keep us out of touch with our feelings, so we have to go contrary to how the world thinks. We women are "feeling" beings and our bodies, emotions, and spirits are adversely affected when we do not express our feelings in a healthy way. Our feeling nature is closely tied into our intuition, so we must learn constructive ways to express these feelings so we more readily tap into this powerful part of us. Intuition lives in your body, so pay attention to what it is telling you. Your body is the first place that your intuition manifests. Learn to trust it. Use this gift that has been given to you.

For many of us, expressing how we feel was contrary to the way we were raised. I believe some of that is changing in the newer generation of young women, as well as in young men. Being a "feeling" person myself, I struggled with my emotions through a good part of my life. During my thirties and forties it became more challenging for me to hold them in. When I did express how I felt, I could see in my husband's and my children's actions that they just plain didn't want to deal with it. I had led them to believe I was a strong woman, and they looked at crying as being weak. Most of my crying ended up in secret.

I never saw my mother cry. She may have cried alone, but I saw her as controlling her feelings, no matter what. So, I was taught to act strong, to endure. As I am writing this, I am crying for my mother because I truly feel she was only following what she had learned a generation earlier. I, personally, feel that it is healthy to have a good cry; it is good for the soul. So, if you are having a difficult day, feeling tense and wanting to run away from it all, give yourself a good cry. Believe me, it is okay to cry even if you don't know what you are crying about because every single tear and burst of crying has some meaning.

Ask yourself what your feelings are telling you. Going deeper into the feeling is always beneficial, but if you just can't handle that at the time, at least release the pent-up emotions. Pound pillows, scream as loud as you can (of course, when you're alone), pound the mattress. . . get it outside of yourself! I am convinced that many, many women are angry, but a facade has been so carefully structured that they don't see through it. And, that facade must be broken if they are to embrace their "authentic self." Don't let unresolved anger result in a life of loneliness, unhappiness, and dissatisfied relationships.

Can we learn to express our anger at the time of an upset or, in some cases, wait until we have thought things through and are more rational? But, then, get it out! Anger is okay as long as it has purpose and is guided toward a positive end. Otherwise it is dangerous and counter-productive.

Some us have been brought up to be "nicey nice" all of the time. I am one of them. But, I have learned it is okay to have anger; it is part of being human. If you have very old anger that has festered for years, be careful you don't take it out on everyone else around you. But, most of all, held-in anger is so destructive to our personal well-being. It actually numbs us to what is going on within ourselves and what is going on with others. Until we allow ourselves to feel the anger when it comes up, we will have problems in our relationships. A lot of the anger women feel is because they do not feel good enough about themselves. Many women sacrifice to get approval and, then, feel used. I certainly have been in that place! Can you see how these kinds of actions result in losing a great deal of our self-worth?

There is one important issue I want to touch on regarding anger, and that is the anger we felt as a child and never expressed in a way to totally release it. So, we are talking now about the feelings of the "child within". . . the lost child who did not get her needs met early in life. Not healing this child within can keep us from having good relationships in our lives now. Those of us who were deeply injured as a young child often become insecure, fearful, and helpless in our marriages. We are still trying to get the love we did not get from one or both of our parents, and we are still trying to please, hoping this will bring us the love we are seeking. I believe it is important to look at whether or not this would be part of your agenda so you can heal this once and for all. You begin by recognizing what is happening and then proceed by being the parent you wanted when you were young. This calls for lots of self-nurturing and a lot of forgiveness to others and to yourself.

We may not be aware of it, but we all do a certain amount of self-parenting within our minds all the time. Self-parenting is a natural component of our thoughts, emotions, and behaviors in life. The old tapes often play over and over again as our self-parenting becomes the overly harsh and critical ways we were brought up. Or, it may be in a simple belief that was drilled into us that keeps us from validating our feelings. We may not remember the actual incidents, but the feelings and beliefs remain within us.

Self Parenting by John K. Pollard is a wonderful book that assists us, first, in understanding what is actually going on in our heads, and then taking us through ways to re-parent ourselves. Once you begin to see the picture of what is happening as a result of your anger and early conditioning, you can begin to build a better life for yourself. We know there are certain inequities in our lives, but let's not make it all someone else's fault. We need to take responsibility for our own lives. If our lives are messed up, we're the ones who have to clean up the mess. That's just the way it is!

Sometimes we hurt inside and are confused by our own feelings. These are the times when we need to comfort ourselves. Please don't criticize yourself for feeling the way you do. This only breaks down the inner spirit. Try to understand where the feeling is coming from and what has triggered it. If you do not have SELF NURTURING on the top of your list of things to do each day, change that. We need to learn to comfort ourselves.

We can begin to avoid covering up our feelings by overeating, popping pills, using alcohol and drugs, overspending, or whatever else we do. These behaviors serve the purpose of covering up the emotional pain that we have not yet learned to deal with. This does not make you a "bad" person; there is just a much better way to get your needs met. And, lashing out at someone else never solves anything. It is fascinating to me to realize that most of us lack the skill to really get into our true feeling nature. I find when I stop myself and say, "What is really going on?", I am able to penetrate through whatever resistance I have built up in not getting down to the real cause of my emotional unrest.

With some women, the issues are very deep and often reveal themselves through addictions. Whatever the addiction is. . . alcohol, drugs, work, food, sex, perfectionism, or overspending. . . it renders you powerless at one degree or another. Your energy is focused on your addiction, thus pulling you away from having a good relationship, and pulling you away from truly loving yourself. Go for help. You will be astonished at how much you will learn in a twelve-step program.

The solution to your problem when addictions are involved is not that the problem go away, but that you come to terms with your own inner struggles and fears. Getting in touch with parts of yourself that feel so very lost will allow you to feel the pain and let the tears come. And, it would be helpful to jot down a few notes concerning your feelings at that time. Our society encourages "quick fixes" for everything, but as we begin to see what we are doing to ourselves and how hurtful it is, we can begin to heal the inner wounds through a healthier and more loving way. The following says it beautifully:

We must learn to awaken and keep ourselves awake,
not by mechanical aids, but by an infinite
expectation of the dawn, which does not
forsake us, even in our soundest sleep.
　—Henry David Thoreau

The more I study and the more I continue to search my heart and my own inner wisdom, the more I see that the feelings we hide are predominantly of NOT FEELING WE ARE GOOD ENOUGH, ABANDONMENT, DISCONTENTMENT WITH OUR WORK, OVERWHELMED FEELING OF HAVING TOO MUCH TO DO, and HELD-IN ANGER AND RESENTMENT. Not dealing with those feelings only accelerates the problem, but we have been brainwashed to think our feelings don't count. They *do* count, and they count in numerous ways that negatively affect our daily lives.

Many relationships are strained, if not broken, due to feelings not expressed. It's time to face the truth, get the support you need, and begin to see that someone has lied to you about your own worthiness. You deserve to be that person you were created to be, and that is always good. Yes, there is healing to be done, but begin now to validate your feelings and know there is a reason you are experiencing the pain and unhappiness.

We can no longer afford to just brush over things that truly matter and say, "Oh, well, that's just the way it is," or "I know I don't deserve anything better, so why try." *Every single one of us has the seed of magnificence in us*. It comes in all shapes and forms, but it is there. Many times it has been covered up so well we think we don't have it, but if you truly want to shine, there is help available to you in so many places.

To ask for help is a wonderful way to tell yourself that you are willing to do *your* part in the search for the real you. I have had so many "New Beginnings" in my life. Some of the changes were disconcerting at first, but I stuck with it because I knew it would become easier as I adjusted to the change, and as I gained more faith in something greater than myself to guide me. There will be many "New Beginnings" as you touch the very essence of who you are, and there will be closures to other things in your life that no longer serve you.

Chapter Three
WOMAN'S SENSE OF FULFILLMENT

I have come to see so clearly that having self-fulfillment is essential if we are to find true meaning in our lives and, more than that, to feel that our very existence is valuable. Are you feeling fulfilled right now? If not, accept that it is possible to make the necessary changes to bring something new into your life; something that will allow you to use your gifts in a most meaningful way. If you are barely getting through the day or your tasks seem meaningless, there is something terribly wrong. Getting in touch with your deepest feelings will help you change that. Be still and allow your feelings to guide you. Let yourself know that you count whether you believe it right now or not.

Learn to speak up for yourself. It will take courage to do this if it is new to you. You may have to go and practice in a mirror before confronting someone. It is important to learn this because it is part of empowering yourself to be all you are meant to be. When you can stand up for yourself, I promise you will feel so good that you will continue to make your feelings and your needs known.

Men often do not understand women's needs. The more you get in touch with your needs, the more you begin to validate yourself. Some of your needs must be met by you, and it is fair to assume that others in your life will also meet certain needs. But, you have to be clear on what those needs are. If you are extremely needy, you may be too dependent on others, and they may feel overburdened by your neediness. Writing down your needs will help to show you more about who you are.

Above all, do not declare war on the men. We are all trying to learn, and hopefully we can do that with a certain amount of caring. You don't have to be compulsive about making changes and turn the whole house upside down. Once you begin to give yourself some quiet time and open yourself up to all the creativity you have been avoiding, you will see parts of yourself that will astonish you. These parts need to be expressed because it is an act of empowering the self, which results in greater self-worth.

As I worked toward more creative expression for myself, I could see how I sabotaged myself by holding on to my old need to be constantly busy, fussing over things that really didn't matter, and needing to always be "productive", a word that had meaning attached to it that said, "Working long and hard is good for you." That belief cut out all possibility of having "quiet time." I never would have written this book if I had not given myself time to touch that part of me that yearned to write and to really believe I could do it. And, I would not have learned to rely on Divine guidance to help me if I had not given myself permission to be still and to listen.

Another way we sabotage ourselves is to stay in unhealthy relationships. We're so busy being angry at our designated other, or others, that we drain most of our energy which in turn prevents us from taking time to get in touch with what is right and good for ourselves.

Don't get too busy to discover who you are. And, don't wear yourself out so you don't even stop for self-nurturing and self-care. I recently went to a funeral of a woman whose son worked for me. She probably was in her late sixties. Family and friends who got up and talked about the woman said how she was there for everyone. . . she never hesitated to help others. In talking with the son at a luncheon given after the service, he said he didn't know how the family could get along because his mother did everything! As I was sharing this with my husband, I wept for this soul who probably never thought about her own needs or had time to do something nice for herself. Audrey Lord states in her book, *A Burst of Light:*

"Overextending myself is not stretching myself. I had to examine in my dreams, as well as in my immune function tests, the devastating effects of over-extension. I had to accept how difficult it is to monitor the difference. Caring for myself is not self-indulgence. It is self preservation."

Don't give until you are depleted and subject to illness.

Not being in touch with who we are and how we express our talents can bring about frustration, depression, and even contribute to some physical illnesses. Think about that statement. I have experienced this in my own life, and I have been able to change behavior that once encouraged illness to reveal itself.

Many women have been trained to meet their husband's and children's needs first, and if there is anything left over it is okay for them to go ahead and give it to themselves. We cook food to please our husbands and children, but often ignore our own likes. We make sure our families get the best and largest piece of whatever we are making, and we even eat the kids' leftovers. Many of us don't even buy ourselves a new outfit because everyone else needs something. We just don't think we're valuable enough to warrant new things that could lift our spirits.

I am not clear about how the younger generation of women feel about this, but I most certainly know without a doubt how it was when I was first married and raising children. I worked outside the home because we needed the money to pay bills, but I was told by my husband in no uncertain terms that I had to figure out how to also take care of the house and the children. I didn't know any better then, so I became "super woman."

That was a long time ago, but some of you may have that same mind-set that you *have to do it all*. It is wonderful to be loving and kind, but don't allow yourself to become that woman who will do everything, not setting boundaries for herself. There is a balance to be established in giving and receiving. If you are compulsive about work you will find this more challenging. Go within and seek out ways to at least "tame" your compulsive habits.

I believe I was able to give a lot to my children, and I never shirked my household duties. I know now that I was tired so much of the time that I may not have given as much as I would have liked. I desperately tried to hold on to my dreams, and by the time I was forty-six years old I was saying, "When is it going to be my turn?" I couldn't see that I would find myself while in the marriage, so I divorced. I knew these feelings had been going on for a long time, and now that my children were grown and leaving the nest, I had to finally make that leap into the unknown.

When you wait too long, it is easy to just stick with it. If you decide to leave, it is painfully difficult letting the family know of your intentions. I felt a lot of guilt over the inadequate ways of telling my own children I was divorcing their father. Knowing what I know today I probably would have done things differently, but I'm quite sure I would not have stayed in the marriage. One thing I know, I never regretted my decision. Again, it was one of those times where the energy was moving, and I thought if I didn't do it then, I probably would stay frustrated, unfulfilled, and resentful.

There are times when we need to tell ourselves "It's my turn." This does not mean you have to leave your husband. And, this does not mean thinking only of yourself. That is unrealistic. It means you have to take full responsibility for the changes you make, and I know that is difficult for a lot of women. This definitely is not a put-down to any woman. Each of us is on our own journey. Some women are at a place where they recognize the need to take responsibility for themselves because it empowers them to do whatever they can to bring meaning and purpose to their lives. And some women are not at that place. Each of us moves through life in our own way. I am not making anyone right or wrong.

I needed to be on my own enough to accept whatever came, and I did just that. It was the stepping-stone for me to have a deep sense of fulfillment and to build on my self-worth. There were a lot of challenges along the way. I have often said, "It is not the challenge itself that is the problem; it is how we are handling it." Well, some days I handled it great and other days not so great. I began to remind myself that I can go through the process of solving my problem by being still and searching my own inner wisdom. It took awhile to slow down enough to even remember to sit and be still.

I had so many wonderful people come into my life who supported me at these times. There are still moments when I question my ability to do something, and I wonder whether or not it is that old feeling lurking around that says, "I don't deserve", or "I can't." When you say you can't, you really mean you won't. I continue to work on my deserving of every good thing and to realize I am co-creator of my life. Our Divine source does not do it all! We are the ones who finally make the choices and take the action. Regardless of how far we think we have come, there is always more. It's a lifetime of waking up, and it's a lifetime of self-discovery.

There is no one out there who can make your life the way you want it. Your dreams and aspirations can become real for you as you rely on your inner wisdom. And, yes, there will be times when you will wonder whether or not you are really receiving the message from your Divine source, or whether your own self-will was imposed. That is just part of the process of learning to trust. As you really search that inner place for guidance, you will begin to know when the message comes forth, and you will trust it. Close your ears to those who say your dreams are unrealistic or silly. Hold on to them for they are the deep yearnings of the soul.

Reaching out to other women will ultimately help us all. We can learn from each other and be supportive links in each other's lives. Embracing other women who are struggling to feel loved and fulfilled is part of our calling. Include women in the battered women's shelters and those from other countries as you send out a thought or a prayer. These women need to know they are cared about by feminine spirits all over the world, and I know they feel our energy when we speak for them. We cannot save them for they must save themselves, but we can send our loving energy to them, even while we are learning more about living our own lives.

Certainly, all of us have reason to think we are less than men. Many generations of women before us have been suppressed and often oppressed. Far too many women still succumb to abuse, afraid even to speak up for themselves. We cannot discount the fact that even though this new generation of women is trying desperately to blow that old image away, it does still exist. We carry the feelings of the women who have gone before us in our minds and in our hearts. And we grieve for those who still do not have enough self-worth to get help for themselves.

However, I feel there is hope for all women to become what they are meant to be because there is a divine purpose for our existence. We can learn to release our fears, anger, and resentment toward those who seemingly hurt us through their actions and their own restrictions in understanding how to nurture and love. We need to release these feelings and free others, as well as ourselves, to move on. Holding on to fear, anger, or resentment keeps us in some form of bondage. These feelings restrict us from ever finding true peace and contentment in our lives.

In today's world we are bombarded with information via the Internet and through the various media, and the use of the intellect is constantly stressed. Women have a natural gift of coming from the heart. Coming from the heart seems like such a simple concept, but if we were to check ourselves out I think we might find we down play it in our attempt to take on masculine traits. We need to emphasize coming from the heart because it is the only way we will find love and peace within ourselves, and the only way we will be able to have healthy relationships.

Certainly, it is very obvious that the entire world is thirsting for the solace of living within the safety and serenity of love and peace which only comes from the heart. Listen to what your heart is telling you. Many men do not feel with their hearts, or at least do not show it. But, we must not compromise what *we* feel and who *we* are. I am not underestimating the need for a strong intellect, but rather pointing out the possible dangers of thinking that the intellect is all-powerful. It takes so much more than the intellect to say what is in your heart. This may seem strange to some of you because our intellect is more easily accepted in today's world, and women have needed to use their intellect to get ahead in business. We have wanted to be accepted in the masculine world. But, we are now ready to show our true colors. . . to speak intelligently *and* from our hearts.

It used to be that people considered you strange if you talked about what the heart was telling you, but that is changing. And, for those who don't know what you are talking about, you can be the teacher. We have much to learn about taking time to be still and consulting the heart. Instead, we put it under a great deal of stress and strain. No wonder more women than ever suffer from heart disease.

Sue Patton Thoele, in her wonderful little book, *The Woman's Book of Spirit*, says,

"For centuries the head has ruled the roost. 'I think

therefore I am' has been the credo of our left brain-
dominated society, and as a consequence, the whole
world is out of balance. Individually and universally,
we need to return to the balance and harmony that
can only be achieved by training our heads to surrender
to the wisdom and compassion of our hearts."

To be truly fulfilled, we will need the mind/heart connection. If you have a job you love but are too exhausted to enjoy your children or other loved ones in your life, the feeling of fulfillment turns into stress and guilt. Something is out of balance. We all need the heart connection, but especially the children. I worked outside of the home while raising my children, but the jobs women entered into at that time were not as stressful as today. Even then, I found that there were periods of time I had to leave a job and be at home, or to just work part time because it was not fair to my children being gone so much. This way I was able to have that fulfillment and yet have meaningful times with my family. I realize all women cannot pick and choose their ideal situations, but when you can, DO IT! Everyone will benefit. When you can't, execute a plan that focuses on some individual time with each of your children. It's important!

I know the feelings of being overwhelmed by a job plus all the many other responsibilities we women take on. At fifty-two years old I was at that place, and more! While my business had supplied me with a lot regarding self-expression and self-worth, I felt a real calling to dedicate my life toward deeper spiritual awareness.

A couple of years earlier, while I was going through my divorce, I had begun to take courses at the Church of Religious

Science. The emphasis of this belief was on how creative we are, how powerful our minds are, and how through the help of Divine Intelligence, we can get in touch with what we are ready to manifest in our lives. More importantly, this belief brought me to a place where I began to have my personal experience with the Divine. Much of what was taught rang very true for me, but I questioned some aspects of this teaching. I needed to seek out what was true for me by going within. As I attended classes, it was not like learning something totally new; it was about confirming a lot of what I already knew deep within me, but needed to express.

As I continued my religious science classes, I became more and more interested in becoming a minister. As my feelings of being overburdened by my business continued, I began to get serious about having more "quiet time", and I became extremely introspective. I was beginning to get those intuitive feelings again. I felt as though something was moving me to make a big change. I have never been a person to jump into things, so I decided to take a ministerial course and see how it felt to me. I had already received over a year's credits toward ministerial certification.

I began to see clearly that my work was to be in some form of the ministry, but I didn't know exactly how. After some heart-wrenching, decision-making months, I surrendered to the calling. I was able to take the courses part time and work part time, so here I was, preparing for another new birth. I sold my business, which was a huge relief. I was amazed how confident I was in making this decision. I never looked back. During the next four years I stayed dedicated to my goal.

During my last year of training, I came to realize I did not want to be a minister of a church. I wanted to work directly with people who were struggling to find themselves and who were ready to make changes in their lives. I wanted to reach out and touch people and sense their pain. I was very frightened over this new vision I had, and didn't know how I might be able to accomplish such a mission. I can see now how surrendering to a Divine Presence brought me through this difficult time.

My pastor had invited Louise Hay, an ordained minister, author, and lecturer to speak one Sunday morning. Her work was about assisting others who were ready to make constructive changes in their lives. She had just written a best-selling book, *You Can Heal Your Life*. Her work included facilitating workshops and seminars for those who were ready to change and willing to take responsibility for themselves. These programs were based on learning to trust in a power greater than ourselves. Louise was also very much involved in helping people with AIDS. Hearing her speak convinced me that I wanted to talk to her about possibly joining her staff, as this type of work was very much in keeping with my own beliefs and desires.

When I graduated from ministerial school, I made an appointment to see Louise, and upon meeting I knew this was the place for me. While she did not have an opening at that time for someone with my background, it didn't take long before I got a call to join the staff. During the years I spent at Hay Institute I was in charge of counseling as well as doing some writing for Louise. As time went by I became the Director of Hay Institute, assisting with workshops and seminars. It was another one of those times where I felt the energy working with me. I learned a lot, and I gave a lot. This was the ministry I was seeking. I began to see how my entire life experiences had been so very beneficial to me, bringing me to a career that constantly challenged me to be more.

Had I been unwilling to change, I would never have had the feelings of self-fulfillment and self-love that I have today. Your experiences will be different, but they will be just right for you. Stay tuned to your heart's desires. They need to be expressed. Being aware of your feelings and asking for Divine guidance are the best ways to get in touch with those deep desires that are yearning to come into full expression. In order to begin the process of more self-awareness and guidance in your own life, it only requires a willingness to change and to take the first step toward action.

Although this is not a self-help book, I have included a few ideas in this book that you may find helpful. It's all been said before; it's just a matter of being ready to change. Tell yourself that you are worth this time to assess your life. No one else can do it for you. It must become a passion for becoming more of who you are. It takes a shifting of the mind from "what everyone else is telling me" to "what does my heart tell me about who I am and what I need"?

We are back to the importance of giving ourselves some "quiet time." Remember to make simple notes during your special time. Some examples: "I'm so tired, I can't think.". . . "I don't feel anything!". . . "I hate my job.". . . "I feel overburdened.". . . "I stood up for myself today.". . . "I felt like crying today, but held it in.". . . "I'm afraid.". . . "I truly want to change.". . . "I feel everyone is against me", "My husband doesn't understand me.". . . "I feel very angry." Allow yourself to feel the feelings. Believe me, we have a tendency to fight back the feelings and plow on. This is why issues get so big, and we find ourselves exhausted and in very critical situations at times.

As you continue this exercise you will begin to see a pattern that needs changing, and you will feel proud of yourself for making even the smallest of adjustments in your attitude, behavior, and every new action you take. It's good to be grateful for even the small changes you make and know that your life is beginning to respond through a different thought process.

There are no quick fixes. There is a process of, first, *understanding* what you need to change, having a *willingness* to change it, *asking for guidance*, and then moving into *action*. Also, having support at this time is critical. In order to bring these new experiences into your life it requires those quiet moments to go within, believing you do have the power to change circumstances in your life. Go about changing step by step, always believing the process of change is already in effect even if you don't have the results yet.

Changing long-term patterns is not easy. You may not have to make a major change, or life may be calling you to change something monumental. In any event, you will be ready for the challenge. This process absolutely brings results, and it is through this success that you will learn to trust yourself. This is a big accomplishment because it is important to trust your ability to release the fear, and to make the proper choices in your life. Letting go of the fear will be easier as you see some positive changes taking place.

More and more I am hearing women talk about preparing themselves for a new awakening. They are saying it is a certain "feeling" they have, but can't describe it. They intuitively know this is a time for the journey within. We, as women, are ready to be empowered through using our feminine nature and balancing out our intellects with our hearts. We don't need to be competitive about it to see how fast we can get there, wherever "there" is. It is a journey, and the journey is all of it; every day and every year, the sorrows and the joys, sometimes even experiences of depression, and the uncertainty that changes often bring. We need to take the whole package and reach out in faith.

I am changing and growing regularly, sometimes a little and other times with a glorious revelation. I check in with my inner wisdom and ask for new awareness about a particular situation that is bringing up some fear. You will discover your own way to activate your inner wisdom. Like anything else, it takes practice. It is easy to get caught up in the mind-set of the world. To stay on course, keep up your "quiet times" where you ask for the Divine guidance to help you in your daily affairs.

The biggest challenge along my own journey has been to cultivate patience and trust. We all know our weaknesses, and we do not change overnight. Just gently remind yourself that your goal is to embrace the qualities that bring you into greater alignment with spirit. It is very important to be kind and patient with yourself as you travel this road toward greater love, compassion, and self-fulfillment.

There seems to be such a restlessness in "woman" today. Part of her wants to explore her talents and her ability to make money, but part of her sees herself in the more feminine role of wife, mother, caretaker, and a very important role as the nurturing force of life. How does she meet all of these demands? The body and mind can take just so much pushing, running, figuring out, and sleepless nights before it sets off the alarm. It is a struggle to balance out her life. Should she let "super woman" take over, or can she learn to balance her life by relying on her inner wisdom? I have watched my own adult children go through this struggle, and I know they are trying desperately to seek out a deeper wisdom within to direct them.

I, personally, do not feel modern technology has always made our lives easier. Rather, I feel it often has us going at an even faster pace so we don't even have time to sit down and think. Many women are overstimulated and overworked to the point of exhaustion. There doesn't seem to be enough time to just sit, go within, and check ourselves out to see what it is we need. Most women I talk with who are in that fast lane of daily living are starved for just one hour alone. Something is desperately wrong! We struggle so to be who we are *not* meant to be. This is not the way to self-fulfillment, and certainly not the way to establish our self-worth, for our very spirits are crying out.

If you are having any feelings at all of being overwhelmed a good deal of the time, stop and get some perspective on what has created this feeling. Sometimes it is just a matter of one or two minor changes, and sometimes it will be a major overhaul job. And, sometimes we have to create a vacuum in order to make room for the new. It is often painful. It seems we'd rather hold on to that which no longer serves us than to feel the temporary discomfort of change.

I am aware how difficult it is going against what society calls normal. But, when we take the time to be still and to really bring into focus what we are doing, we will be able to see clearly what needs to be changed. Take a good look at whatever is keeping you from your full potential. Why is it so difficult to accept the changes? Check out what your heart is saying for it will tell you the truth. Don't wait until you are faced with a crisis to take the necessary steps toward finding true fulfillment for yourself.

For women who are just plain bored, believe me, there is so much you have not explored about yourself. Even though we sometimes have good intentions to start a new project, change a job, or get some professional help, fulfillment often is lost because there are so many conflicts which are hidden within our minds and our hearts. But, it is never too late to create something new. What a loving act it would be to give yourself the gift of greater self-fulfillment and self-worth.

Creating something new brings in all kinds of new energy. Once you open up to this new energy, you will wait with anticipation for each day in order to release your new-found creative endeavors. Yes, you may have some limitations, but that doesn't mean you can't be creative. Sitting and hoping something will come along won't do it. You are the one who must decide whether or not you want to change your life.

While I have done quite a bit of writing, I have stuffed most of it in drawers for the day when another nudge would move me. And, I have written for other people. Now, I am giving the gift to "me." I can only describe my feelings as pure joy. Was it easy to do this? Absolutely not! My inclination was to abandon the project. But, I knew better, so I started the process of discipline. . . I was saying "yes" to my objective, knowing there was a prize. (I wrote about a meaning of discipline in Chapter one, "Woman's Search for Self.")

I sat down at my computer, put my fingers on the keys, and called out for help to make a beginning. Once my fingers got going, all sorts of ideas came bursting out of me. Yes, there were many changes to be made and days I just needed to be quiet. But, I had a sense of fulfillment with each page I wrote. Every one of you has a gift to give. It may not be writing, but you have something special within you that wants to express itself. Maybe it is doing volunteer work or fulfilling an old desire to draw or paint.

Women who have chosen to be homemakers have all kinds of ways to fulfill themselves. Your gift may be gardening, baking, decorating, or even going into business for yourself right there in your home. I think that homemaking alone can be an extremely satisfying role for many women, and as far as I am concerned it is way underrated. Every woman who dedicates herself to the homemaking role should receive many praises for her acts of love, and definitely should be taken out to dinner from time to time, without first having to ask. No man could ever do what a woman does in her day-to-day activities running a smooth household. God bless our homemakers!

Do you ever catch yourself thinking you are at last on the pathway to positive change only to find a slight hitch in the outcome? Well, join the group. This book is not about reaching perfection or finding the absolute right solution to every problem. It is about doing the best we can, just for now. It's about finding more self-fulfillment and some peace in our lives even during the difficult times. We may have to try various means of finding that fulfillment, but peace and contentment will come to us as we slow down and consciously seek it. It's also about loving and being loved. It's about being in touch with something within us that is far greater than ourselves that sustains us and guides us during periods of change and turmoil.

And, it's about every woman feeling safe, understanding who she is at the deepest level of her being. It's about "woman" joining in with her innate wisdom and love to find that place in her heart where she will remember to say a prayer for every single woman on this planet. We need to be here for each other, to share from our hearts what has worked or not worked for us. I know many of you support friends and family in wonderful ways. But, there are many women who need your prayers as they find ways to pull themselves out of very harmful situations and to see themselves as empowered beings. As we find ways to express our own gifts, we will automatically want to bring hope and support to other women.

Let's all work toward getting rid of our illusions, our procrastinations, our fears, and our denials so we can create a life truly worth living. There are signs that we are going in the right direction, but if we don't give ourselves time for inner reflection and guidance, we stray from our purpose and, ultimately, we are disillusioned, fearful, angry, and just plain exhausted. Our challenges in relationships, money, work, and addictions are only an outer reflection of our inner struggle. To work just on the outer is like putting a band aid on the problem. It might soothe for awhile, but the same problem will surface again until we get down to the true cause.

We all need to do some restructuring of our lives, working from the inside out. This sets the stage for getting in touch with how we can best deal with our challenges. It provides us with new energy to meet our busy schedules. It is up to us to create something meaningful in our lives; something that will bring us a sense of purpose. We would like immediate solutions to our problems, but my experience tells me that it is in the "quiet time" we give ourselves, and in the emotional pain we allow ourselves to feel and move through, that we make a huge step up in creating a meaningful life. Somehow, we are dying to the old, only to be reborn.

With the many new technologies, and the desire to have more, I believe we are in danger of losing something very precious. The more we look to the outer world for happiness, the more disillusioned we become because no matter how much we get of something, it is never enough. Therein lies the illusion. In the end, we are stressed out, and when there is extreme stress, there is danger of illness. At these times, addictive behavior often looms up at the first sight of losing control, and the problems are compounded. I believe we have become a society of addicts in one way or another, and the differences lie in how destructive they are in our lives.

The addictive system fears emotional expression, so it seeks to control the emotions at all cost because it is so out of touch with them. Remaining unconscious about what we are actually feeling takes a great emotional and physical toll on our bodies and spirits. These addictive habits keep us from connecting with our inner wisdom, and they keep us in a state of pain that increases the longer we deny them. Therefore, it is almost impossible even to recognize when our bodies and spirits call out to us.

It is becoming quite apparent to me that much of our entire society functions in ways that keep us out of touch with what we feel. This is why I advocate having "quiet time" so we get in touch with our inner wisdom and allow our deeper feelings to surface. Only then can we begin to heal.

CHAPTER FOUR

OUR NEED FOR LOVE AND GREATER SELF-WORTH

Everyone wants to feel loved. Throughout the ages we have sought love in a variety of ways, according to what we believed love was and according to our needs. We have sometimes frantically looked for love because we were so depleted of love from within. Many of our spirits were injured early in life and the journey to wholeness has been painful. But, what seems to arise out of all of this is how we somehow forgot how to love ourselves. When we are unable to value ourselves as a person, this belief allows destructive forces to invade our very spirits, pulling us down helplessly.

All kinds of addictions begin to surface. Addictions narrow the mind and disable the will. In other words, addicts are out of control. Their lives no longer are conscious choices as everything is built around the addiction. Many, many men and women are trying to find out who they are under the pain and control of addictive behavior. The self-image is often crushed and lives become unmanageable. The various twelve-step programs that emerged taught people to seek out their higher power, take responsibility for their lives, find value in themselves, make amends to those they have hurt, and help other addicts.

It is not only the people who experience addictions lacking self-worth. Many, many women are searching for greater worth in themselves as a result of the belief that women just aren't good enough. Society has perpetuated this belief for a long time, but we are finally ready to change that through understanding more about our own individual self-worth and making better choices in our lives.

I suspect self-worth must precede loving the self because it is far easier to obtain at least a small measure of self-worth than it is to truly love ourselves. Self-worth is having confidence in ourselves. It is self-respect, and that includes respecting our strengths and our weaknesses. It is feeling worthy of good relationships, worthy of praise and worthy of having certain material things that make our lives easier and more enjoyable. In order to establish greater self-worth we need to feel good about our participation in life. We need to recognize our own abilities and to give back to life. Without self-worth we cannot act on our intuitive hunches because there is still too much fear of failure and fear of the unknown.

Working on self-love is different. Here we explore who we are beneath the facades, and we learn to love the very essence of ourselves. We become mature in understanding ourselves and willing to go deeper within to see ourselves in a new way. True self-love demands we know who we are. As we develop a greater sense of self, our intuitive voice becomes heard and it guides us to our next step of unfoldment. By using our intuition we are able to make decisions more easily. Some people seem to think intuition is having the ability to foretell the future. This is misinformation. Intuition is part of our inner guidance system to help us follow through on the feelings we are having concerning change, and to follow through on the hunches. Intuitive guidance helps us to recognize the discomfort or confusion we may be having, and to see that it is actually trying to pull us out of a rut we are in and to move us into new ways of thinking about our lives.

When we can begin to love ourselves, it opens the door for more love to enter. Our daily behavior indicates that we all fall short of being good to ourselves. The ultimate in loving ourselves is to absolutely cherish who we are, and this doesn't mean conceit. It means we care deeply about ourselves, that we have faith in ourselves, and that we have faith in our higher power to help us through the challenges of our everyday existence. It means we automatically will be able to handle our relationships better. It means we are able to listen to what our heart is telling us and that includes listening to our wounded child within and embracing her. It means giving her permission to pour out her heart to you.

Loving ourselves means nurturing ourselves instead of waiting for someone else to come along to do it for us. After much practice, I now feel pure ecstasy when I nurture myself. I know what makes me feel good. It might be gentle stroking of my face or arms, holding my face in my hands and saying, "You are so precious," or it may be a long, hot bubble bath. And often it is just allowing myself to sit and do nothing. Of course, it is always permissible to give ourselves lots of hugs. I find we can give ourselves all the pampering we want and quit expecting it to come from others. We can love ourselves the way we have yearned to be loved because we know exactly what we need, and it doesn't take very much time. We just have to love ourselves enough to do it. The benefits are enormous because others will love us even more.

Touching ourselves is a wonderful way to feel good about

who we are. Touch is a language whereby you communicate more love in five seconds than speaking words for five minutes. Touching is loving and healing. I used to be so busy taking care of everyone else that it didn't even occur to me that I could nurture myself in so many ways. It takes changing some of our priorities, and you have to let people know that you are ready to do this so they don't expect you to do for them things they are most likely very capable of doing for themselves.

This is not selfish. Extremely loving and caring people often feel guilty if they are not doing for others all of the time. Remember, you are important! Slow down, and give yourself time for resting and thinking about what it is you find fulfilling, exciting, and enjoyable in your life. And, when you take good care of yourself you will find time to give to others in a much richer way. Regardless of how much you work on loving yourself, new ideas will come to you as you begin to truly value who you are.

Few of us know how to adequately care for our bodies, acknowledge the yearnings of our spirits, and give ourselves some of the simple pleasures of life. In many cases, the seed of shattered self-worth has been deeply planted, but we can begin to repair our emotional injuries. This chapter has self-helps in it because loving ourselves is not that simple if you have been taking care of everyone except yourself, or if you have carried around a lot of emotional pain for a long time. Many of you have made great strides in loving yourselves, and others are struggling with the very basics of how to go about it.

The various forms of media are good at making us think they have the solutions to our problems by suggesting we can find the perfect mate, the perfect job, and an abundance of money if we buy this product or join that particular group, or whatever. We end up saying, "If I lose weight, I will find love." "If I wear this designer label, I will be accepted by my peers." "If I had a better job, I could love myself." "If I had the perfect boyfriend or husband, I would certainly love myself." This approach never works because the feeling of loving ourselves must come from within. It is merely accepting what spirit already knows about us.

By nature we are all lovable, so if you doubt your lovability, someone has been deceiving you, and that person could be "you." Maybe you have tried to follow society's rules, but they don't work for you. Society uses totally different standards in measuring whether or not you are pretty or whether or not you are lovable. They measure the externals and not the inner beauty of us. In our present society we are overfed, overstimulated, overmedicated, and overworked. *How in the world can we find ourselves through all of this?* We must use the spiritual connection; otherwise we are subject to the beliefs and whims of our society.

The journey of going within is of utmost importance in learning more about ourselves; what our needs are and realizing how lovable we are. Going within is a simple way to quiet yourself and be open to your feelings. It is a time to ask for Divine guidance in all that you do. If you are extremely tired, you may doze off at this time. That is okay, but if you do it a lot you may require more sleep or you may be avoiding change. If you go consistently without proper rest, it affects your life adversely in many ways, and it is not being loving to yourself.

There is no simple instruction for being able to quiet yourself. You have to take a serious look at your life and decide whether or not you want to change. Having a strong motivation for improving your life is of utmost importance. Having "quiet time" is mainly for touching that deeper part of yourself which can help you discover more about who you are. You have to ask yourself the question whether or not you are willing to slow down enough to get in touch with that which can transform your life. In counseling sessions with clients I often would suggest they write down ten things about themselves that they thought were lovable; whatever first came to their minds. You may choose to do this exercise. If you have difficulty finding lovable traits in yourself, you *know* you need to work on loving yourself.

This is not about sharing an overblown ego; nor is it a test on how perfect we are. It is about what you believe about yourself, and how you see yourself. This belief is planted deep in your subconscious mind, and you will act out according to these beliefs. You need to understand this so you can begin to change your belief about how loving you really are, and also how you deserve to be loved. Healthy self-worth and a deep sense of loving yourself gives you entry to unlimited possibilities for a creative and fulfilling life and greatly adds to your own personal happiness.

All of this may sound well and good, but the question is, "How do you make the necessary changes in your thinking and actions to feel this loving toward yourself?" Just for today, take note of what you are thinking, feeling, and how you are acting. Jot a few notes down right now so you will see what pattern of thinking you live by. If you are willing to take responsibility for your life and take some form of action in making positive changes, you are off to a great start. Be kind, gentle, and loving to yourself during these changes. Use an affectionate name such as "honey", "sweetheart", or a nickname. I continue to call myself "honey" especially when I feel discouraged or I am having a "downer" day. This alone is an act of loving the self.

Here are a few things I concentrated on in order to help me recognize my own inner struggles with feeling good about myself:

I BEGAN TO STOP RUSHING - This one took me a long, long time. I knew I couldn't act lovingly to myself and others when I was rushed so much of the time. I know this is a problem in our society today.

I BECAME AWARE OF WHEN I WAS CRITICAL OF MYSELF AND OTHERS - I never, ever, criticize myself anymore. It only breaks down the inner spirit and I end up losing faith in myself. It is definitely not compatible with love.

I CONTACTED MY INNER CHILD AND LET HER KNOW I WAS LEARNING TO TAKE BETTER CARE OF HER. You will immediately feel great emotion at this time. This is a beautiful act of loving yourself.

I MADE A LIST OF PEOPLE I NEEDED TO FORGIVE, AND I REMEMBERED TO FORGIVE MYSELF FOR NOT BEING ALL I WANTED TO BE OR ALL I WANTED THEM TO BE.

DURING MY "QUIET TIME" I ALLOWED MYSELF TO GET IN TOUCH WITH MY FEELINGS. If I felt under pressure, not appreciated, or overly tired, I let the tears flow.

I BEGAN TO ACCEPT ALL OF MYSELF; MY STRENGTHS AND MY WEAKNESSES.

It doesn't take a lot of time to do these things, but it does take a commitment to give your attention to a new way of looking at your life. If you don't stop long enough to see what you are doing, you will never change anything. Check out your body. . . what is it telling you? There are many mental and emotional causes for discomforts that could turn into a serious illness. Ignoring bodily discomforts is not a loving act. When you have chronic pain in the shoulders, indigestion, headaches, foot pain, or a multitude of other symptoms, these are signals of some imbalance in your system.

Your body is telling you something is wrong. Instead of running for a pill or relying on food or alcohol to cover up what really needs to be healed, be still and ask yourself what the real problem is. Are you angry with someone? Are you working too many hours? Do you feel overwhelmed a good deal of the time? More people than ever have feelings of lone-liness, alienation, isolation, and depression, and these feelings are not primarily with older people. What will it take to show us that we are all spiritually undernourished?

Certainly, I am not saying I have all the answers, but in my own life I know that until I dealt with my inner self and trust-ed a greater power to help me change certain beliefs and pat-terns of living, I continued to cover up my discomforts. Medical science is not going to come up with the cure for courses of action we take that are harmful to ourselves. They may be able to give us medication for the symptom, but they are not going to make the problem go away. They can only cover up the symptoms with medication or possibly surgery. We need to get in touch with what we are feeling and what we are believing.

Most of the ways in which I participated in my own heal-ing are in this book. I do not know what you need. If you iden-tify with some of the things I have written about, begin to make some changes before you are faced with a greater crisis.

Until we get to the point where we have had enough of the things that hurt, and begin to seek out greater understanding, love, and forgiveness, we are doomed to take painful roads. It's time to go beyond the quick fixes.

Using simple affirmations about loving ourselves is helpful in counteracting the stress that builds up, but they must be used consistently, such as: "I am learning to slow down."; "I am becoming more aware of my feelings."; "I am ready to listen to what my heart is telling me."; "I am learning to feel more love toward myself."; "I am willing to give myself quiet time." These affirmations alone are not going to completely change your life, but it will help to take this simple form of action in order to empower the emotional body to seek out what mental patterns are triggering you. If you are on the "go" most of the time, it will require you to slow down and perhaps get some professional help. This book will help you if you take the time to do some of the exercises I have suggested and give yourself some "quiet time."

I know many of you very much want to change. Changing some of your beliefs and learning to love yourself requires making a commitment. The more you work with changing your thinking, the more your affirmations become true for you. I found that quiet contemplation helped me to bring new thoughts to reality because I acquired a deeper understanding of what I believe. A definition of "contemplation" is : *to view or consider with continued attention.* Insight and wisdom often come from true contemplation, but it won't come if you are totally stressed out. As you continue contemplating, you will notice a shifting in your thinking and a shifting in your body. When the mind once makes a change, the body will follow.

I don't know about you, but I used every coping mechanism imaginable before I allowed myself to look deep into my feelings. My body gave me all kinds of signals that change was called for. I made a giant step in the direction of loving myself when I began to ask myself the following questions:

1 - How do I view myself on a day-to-day basis?
2 - Do I feel less than those I work with or less than my friends or family?
3 - Do I resist change?
4 - Am I always seeking approval?
5 - Do I believe that someone or something outside of myself can hurt me?
6 - Do I trust myself to make good decisions?
7 - Am I willing to let go and allow a higher power to reveal what is best for me at this time?
8 - Can I see beyond looks and personality to the gifts I have been given?

If you answer "yes" to most of these questions, you need to love yourself more. These questions are not about being good or bad. But, they are about the very core of you and about finding your greater self-worth and inner joy. They are to help you understand what you are feeling and what you are believing.

Tune into the idea that you are part of something far greater than yourself that is here to help you. We are not meant to "go" it alone. Above all, comfort yourself during the challenging times. The goal is always to be loving to yourself. If you find that difficult, it is because you have bought into what others have said, and it was not true. Even well-meaning parents often instill in their children ideas that translate into "I'm not good enough." You are worth loving! If you wait until "mommy" or "daddy" change and make everything okay, you may wait forever. If you keep trying to change your husband so he will love you more, it may never happen.

Take control of your thoughts as you build on your self-love. Treat yourself in a loving and kind way and those new habits you establish for yourself will be noticed by those around you. Love begets love. Sometimes just a simple word such as "stop" can buy you enough time to let go of a fear. Or say, "I am not willing to do this any longer." That is a powerful statement! However you approach this, always remember that you are worth feeling good about yourself, and you are worth having a loving and fulfilling life.

And, please don't be hard on yourself because you haven't understood some of these ideas earlier. Perhaps you were not ready earlier, but now is the time to look at yourself in a completely different way; to understand that you are now ready to place greater value on yourself. This is how you empower yourself to make better choices.

Loving ourselves is synonymous with learning to trust ourselves. Through the years as I continued to work on loving myself more. . . and there is always more. . . I posed these questions when I made choices: Is this decision motivated by love for myself? And, that doesn't mean just getting my own way. Am I willing to accept the consequences of this choice? If either of the answers were "no", I would give myself "quiet time" and re-think how to make a better decision.

I know it is difficult to change old behavior, but it can be done. We cannot learn to trust ourselves if we continue to make unhealthy choices in our lives. Every time you choose something of real value for yourself. . . and it doesn't have to be something big. . . you boost your self-worth and your self love.

Again, I emphasize that loving ourselves requires making a commitment, and it often requires us to slow down and to let go of our unfounded fears. When we are able to make some positive decisions, we will gain trust in ourselves, and that most certainly is a loving act. If we don't change the way we approach a decision and just hope it all will turn out okay, we set ourselves up for failure.

Not valuing our own person, our own ideas, and our own abilities keeps us from seeing our "authentic self." We are so accustomed to believing other people's opinions rather than our own that we have come to doubt our ability to know anything of value or to believe that we have anything of importance to say. Sometimes, we even go as far as trusting other people's opinions of who we are. If you are a "people pleaser," get to the bottom of why you are willing to withhold from yourself in order to please someone else. It's too big a job to try and make everyone else happy! Tell yourself that it is time to take charge of your own life and that you are important enough to begin pleasing yourself.

It is scary at first to make such changes because you haven't learned how to make your own decisions and you doubt your own worthiness. And, many of us don't give to ourselves because we haven't been taught it is okay. But, like anything else, you practice, practice, practice, and pretty soon you get better at it. This does not mean you will no longer be a "giving" person. It just means you no longer give until the well is dry.

And, you most certainly will learn that you must guard against being a caretaker or enabler to a practicing alcoholic or drug addict. Other addictions may bring that out in you too where you feel responsible to help these people realize what they are doing. This can be an over-responsibility issue and you will wear yourself out trying to change those who may be in denial. They need to seek out help through a twelve-step program. I could write a whole book about this from experience because I have been there, and I *did* wear myself out. When our personalities lend themselves to being overly kind and loving to people, we need to see whether or not we are crossing the line into territory that says we are enabling someone by doing for them what they need to be doing for themselves.

You are special with your own unique gifts. Learn to accept this about yourself. You don't need to be like someone else. This is negating your own person, and at some level of your being you are saying, "I don't love who I am." As we find worth in ourselves and see ourselves through the eyes of unconditional love, we no longer have to be the victim.

Learning to love ourselves unconditionally is a lifetime process. It is important to explore the various parts of ourselves, identifying how each serves us, including those which act as restrictors. It may require looking at a part of ourselves that we don't like. We all have character defects. . . we all have a dark side to our personalities. It is unrealistic to think we can immediately love all of these parts of ourselves. We must take the journey of greater understanding and compassion. This is not about excluding all concern for others. When we love ourselves, we automatically love others as well. But, while we are learning this we must be diligent about first caring for ourselves.

Know that whatever challenges you are going through

right now, you can turn them into an opportunity for self-growth and self-worth. Some of you have had very hurtful experiences. Even in cases of sexual abuse, incest, and battering; with professional help, one can begin to understand that the perpetrators of such actions are extremely sick people, and that you did the best you could in that situation. It takes having a new perspective rather than staying a victim. I realize these hurts go very deep, but do not underestimate the power of spiritual healing.

Working with Louise Hay, I learned the visualization of seeing a person who had deeply hurt me as a small child and putting him into my heart. I, then, put myself right next to him. We hold each other, and I make known my desire to forgive him. I suddenly felt great compassion for this person. This is a powerful tool to use in situations that are so very difficult to release. The image of a child is used in this exercise because most of us can relate to a small child who needs love. It takes a lot of energy to hold on to harmful memories and feelings. Make this the time to direct your energies into something that will heal and bring out the "authentic you."

We all have certain lessons to learn in this earth experience, and I hope the things I am writing about will help you to move through your challenges and reap the gift of a life filled with love, compassion, and understanding. As you begin to build a greater sense of self-worth and self-love, you will find new people coming into your life who are also on the path of making positive changes, and you can support each other as you move through your new experiences.

We are all learning to love ourselves more because the more we uncover, the more we see possible. Some of you have built a wall around yourself and love cannot enter. But, that doesn't mean you can't tear that wall down right now. We all have much to learn about loving. Be patient and kind to each other and use this time in your lives to talk to each other, to hold each other, to be honest with each other, and to allow the love you are building within yourself to create a whole new world for you. Love is always the answer.

Another activity I have found most helpful is mirror work. It had never occurred to me to look myself straight in the eyes and say, "I love you, Hara." While assisting with seminars and workshops with Louise Hay, we always had that activity. I was absolutely astonished how many of the participants could not do this exercise. I have noticed when challenges come up, in my own life, I am in need of letting the child within *me* know that she is loved. If I went to the mirror at these times, looked myself straight in the eyes, and announced to myself how much I loved myself, I was amazed at how I immediately felt better. I also would ask myself what I was feeling. This usually brought up some very important things that I needed to work at.

I use mirror work to this day when life is challenging me in some way. If you find it difficult to do this exercise, I encourage you to stay with it. This is a powerful tool to help you learn to love yourself in a way you never imagined possible. The following was partially taken from "The Guy in the Glass," author unknown.

THE GAL IN THE GLASS

When you get what you want in your struggle for self,
And the world makes you Queen for a day.
Just go to a mirror and look at yourself,
And see what THAT reflection has to say.

For it isn't your father, mother or husband
whose judgment upon you must pass;
The person whose verdict counts most in your life
Is the one staring back from the glass.

Some people may think you a trusting ole gal
And call you the best alive,
But the gal in the glass says you're just not good enough
If you can't look her straight in the eye.

She's the one to please, never mind the rest
For she's with you clear up to the end,
And you've passed your most dangerous, difficult test
If the gal in the glass is your friend.

You may fool the whole world down the pathway of years
And get pats on the back as you pass,
But your final reward will be heartaches and tears
If you've cheated the gal in the glass.

Woman's Journey To Wholeness

CHAPTER FIVE
CHANGE

The world continues to change; nothing is stagnant. We are all part of a process which has its cycles, and it appears this is a time we all need to make positive changes so that we are in harmony with the universal changes. Some of the changes you may be experiencing are in the death of a loved one, relationships, health, work, money, or addictions. I know from my own experience that when I perceive change to be difficult, I do a certain amount of moaning and groaning, creating some anxiety for myself. I know better, but my all-too-human nature comes out, and there I am having to *again* look at what I say I believe.

I vividly recall when I was forced to leave a job because the department I headed closed down. I was shocked and frightened. I had recently bought a townhouse close to my work and debated whether or not I would be able to keep it. I was sixty-two years old at the time and eligible for early social security. The real estate market was spiraling down, but putting large sums of money toward a mortgage was beginning to give me some pangs of fear. I was still unmarried, and so I was forced to look at how secure I really was as I made this decision.

I had all of this knowledge in my head about every challenge can be turned into an opportunity, and now I had to apply it to my personal life. Sometimes it was even difficult stopping and asking for Divine guidance because I allowed fear to enter. I knew how easy it was to make poor choices when I was fearful. I used prayer and meditation in order to counter that fear. Within six months I made the decision to sell, get early retirement and move to a rental house I owned. I took a huge loss on this sale, but something within me assured me it was the right thing to do. I couldn't even allow myself to think of the physical move.

I reminded myself to keep calm and just take a step at a time. All of this was a test in trusting. There are three things I kept clearly in my mind:

1 - *Ask for Divine guidance*
2 - *Take some form of action*
3 - *Trust the outcome will be good*

I understood the necessity to let go of any particular outcome. This is part of the trusting. The scenario of "I want what I want, and I want it now." cannot be part of the agenda.

I had just met the man who is my husband today, and he was a big help to me in so many ways. He assisted me in my move and gave me a lot of moral support. Once settled into my new home, I began to do private counseling, and I also did writing for Louise Hay, for whom I had worked. I felt good in my old, but charming house, and I blessed every inch of it. It was in an area way down from what I was used to, but I didn't dwell on that. I just gave thanks. This experience taught me a lot about moving through change by seeing beyond the immediate picture.

I sought out the things to be grateful for instead of being unhappy about where I was living. I felt I had made the right decision, and it proved to be a wonderful part of my personal growth. You can paint a doomsday picture or you can create something good. It really is up to you! It's imperative that you do not allow fear to take over. You can be realistic about how your needs will be met without paralyzing yourself with fear. An immense amount of energy is used by practicing fear and negativity. There is something about moving through a big challenge that fortifies one for life if we truly work on releasing our fears. It is not enough to read about ways to help us through the tough times. The real teacher is the experience itself because nothing is truly learned until it is lived.

I am confident that somewhere in the seed of change is the opportunity for self-growth. For me, it's been as though spirit was calling out to me to be more. Our challenge is to answer the call. If we want to move forward, we have to be flexible and willing to change, knowing we are supported by life itself, and that we are creative beings able to do much more than we think we can.

In the midst of change there is often turmoil. I have found that it is best to accept the uneasy feelings and, yes, sometimes there are storms that rock the very foundation of our being. Trust me, these are the times our faith in something greater than ourselves is tested to the limit. These are the most valuable lessons of all!

One reality I have seen very clearly in my own life, and with the many individuals I have worked with, is most people are uncomfortable with change. Many are so paranoid about change that when something challenging comes up, they panic and immediately scramble to do something that will just make the feeling of terror go away. In many instances relationships are terminated, overeating looms big, bad decisions regarding money are made, and fear keeps them from moving through the experience with faith that a higher source of intelligence is available to them. If all else fails, maybe they will finally see there is a gentler way to take care of this challenge. By being still and allowing our inner spirit to give us clues on what steps we need to take, we will rid ourselves of the fears that keep us from preparing for the change.

I admit there have been times when it was most difficult for me to know whether or not I should take a certain action, but I allowed myself to have some doubts. After all, we are human! Sometimes I would have to quiet my mind by letting go of concerns that sometimes popped up. And, yes, sometimes my decisions were not so good. But, the key is in asking for Divine guidance in all that we do. When we change inwardly, we are able to see more clearly the beliefs and patterns that have kept us from being all we are meant to be.

Know that the journey continues, so don't beat yourself up by thinking you did not make a good enough choice. Experience is the best teacher, however painful it might be. Use whatever choice you made to learn more about yourself. Check to see whether or not you are repeating a harmful pattern over and over again.

Be assured that your life will bring change because it is a law of nature. And, as a law of nature, we have it within us to handle the change. We think we know what is good for us, but we rarely do. The experiences we put ourselves through are often exhausting, but some of us have had to learn the hard way. Let's learn from our mistakes and move on.

Acknowledge the fear, anger, disappointment or hurt that you are feeling while going through difficult changes, but remind yourself what a creative being you are. Get some kind of a support system while you are going through big changes, and know somewhere within you are the answers for all of life's challenges. It is too much to think we must do all of this alone. Your inner guidance may point you to a new friend, a support group, a church, or you may find help in a book.

The greatest thing I have learned to help me through "change" is to nurture myself and to trust that my Divine source is activating something within me to help make the change in a positive way. If something from the past is triggering fear *in you*, acknowledge the fear, but consciously release its hold on you. In the case of a divorce or separation, check out to see whether or not the fears you are feeling are triggered by events of your younger years. If you have not been able to get your needs met through the various relationships you have had, look to see whether or not this is a feeling you have carried for a long time.

It is my personal belief that the only way we can change negative feelings that pop up unexpectedly is to deal with the wounded child within. Even as adults, part of us is still that little child from long ago who needs to feel loved and accepted. I recently read a wonderful book for people who have had painful childhoods, *Legacy of the Heart*, by Wayne Muller. It is one of the most compassionate books I have ever read on this subject. It offers a whole new perspective on how we can view the hurtful events from the past. He writes,

> *"We are not broken; childhood suffering is not a*

moral wound, and it did not irrevocably shape your
destiny. Your challenge is not to keep trying to repair
what was damaged; your practice instead is to
reawaken what is already wise, strong, and whole
within you, to cultivate those qualities of the heart
and spirit that are available to you in this very moment."

These words bring to us a sense of hope. We all need to awaken to that inner strength in us regardless of our past because this is where we will discover a sense of safety, belonging, and peace. We change our friends, our spouses, our homes, our jobs, always hoping this will be the answer to our problems, and it rarely is. The wounds often linger because they have become so deep we don't even realize they are there. But, we are living evidence that something needs to be healed. It is time to move beyond the fears and the emotional pain of the past.

We are all living in a time of vast change in all phases of our lives. How can we counter the stresses, find meaning in our lives, and learn how to get rid of the guilt for wanting to create something special for ourselves? I believe the answer lies in letting go of a lot of excess baggage; of getting a sense about why we are here, and about expressing our true nature to the best of our ability. We, as women, need to gather together and support each other as we face some of life's challenges.

I believe we are on the threshold of a new way of looking at ourselves. Take special notice of the powerful women today. Oprah Winfrey is one who definitely comes from the heart. She has contributed so much to women as they search for deeper meaning in their lives. There are so many role models today who can encourage us to be "more." Powerful women are willing to tell their stories in order to help other women. They are willing to share their pain, how they transformed that pain by forgiving, and how they came to discover more of who they are. As you make positive changes in your own life, other women will notice.

Read books where you can learn about women's issues. The bookstores and libraries are filled with books about women who have overcome great challenges through real soul searching. Be willing to make some changes in your life now.

It is so easy to take our pain, boredom, and inflexibility out on others. This only locks us into the same old results we have been having that are so dissatisfying. We really have to learn to take responsibility for ourselves and that can be frightening. Taking responsibility for ourselves includes looking at our thoughts, our attitudes, and our willingness to change. Once we accept personal responsibility for even one or two areas of our lives we can no longer blame someone else. At this point we often need to establish new relationships that support the new direction we are going in our lives.

I hope something in this book will help you to begin some kind of a program for yourself. You may even want to start a discussion group in your home. However you decide to approach change, begin with something small so you don't get overwhelmed. I know it is possible to overcome some of your earlier beliefs because I have done it. I know it is possible to learn to trust yourself and to love and appreciate yourself because I have done it. So, don't give up! You only have to begin with a willingness and intention to change. Then, give yourself some "quiet time" to get in touch with what you are feeling. This is immensely important! Life is about change. It encompasses:

LEARNING TO TAKE A DAY AT A TIME
OVERCOMING FEAR

FORGIVING

TRUSTING OUR HIGHER POWER

LETTING BARRIERS DOWN SO LOVE CAN COME IN.

SETTING BOUNDARIES FOR OURSELVES

USING OUR CREATIVE TALENTS

I believe one of the most important changes is in health care. We really *can* learn to take better care of ourselves, to give ourselves time for reflection and self-nurturing. If we do this, we will be in touch with what our bodies are telling us.

The body loves to be pampered. The cells in our body are intelligent; they know when the body is taken care of and when it is ignored. It seems we need to have a whole new outlook on our bodies, as well as the whole of our being. To some of you, this may sound strange. But, if you stop and think about how you treat your body, you may want to take heed to what I am saying. It doesn't matter where you are right now in your life. Just begin to make a commitment to learn more about yourself; your feelings, your needs, your desires, your talents, and yes, even your disappointments.

Learn to be your own best friend. If you continue your "quiet times," eventually you will learn to trust your inner feelings, the *nudges* and the *ah-ha's*. You need to act on those feelings. There are no shortcuts to becoming a whole person. But, once you really get to know yourself and work toward establishing greater confidence in yourself, the journey becomes easier. It's sometimes hard work discovering who we are, to understand why we want to continue blaming, why we hold on to the addictions, and why we dislike change so much. We're actually creating a new identity for ourselves. It's a whole new way of thinking and living our lives.

There are changes that take place in our lives that we have

no control over. Weather patterns change, technology changes are coming fast and furiously, loved ones die, divorces shake us up, people fear losing their jobs, relationships are tested, and illness often comes. We are all struggling to live our daily lives within the framework of some of these changes. Each of us is growing and changing, and that alone can bring some conflicts as we search for stability in our lives.

The good news is being in control of your life makes you a powerful woman because you have developed self-understanding, independence and self-respect. Life flows so much easier when you are confident in yourself and able to connect with the creative energies within you. Yes, this takes time and energy, but once you change the things you can, you must ride with the rest. I love the Serenity Prayer that the twelve-step programs use: *"God, grant me the serenity to accept the things I cannot change, the courage to change the things I can, and the wisdom to know the difference."*

I have had a tremendous amount of change in my life; some very difficult and some amazingly easy. The easy ones came as I learned to trust myself more. The changes in my childhood were horrendous, moving every other year because we couldn't pay the rent. My father could not hold down a job and succumbed to drink. He abandoned my mother several times. Finally, my mother divorced him. She had five children to take care of. I felt what I know now as shame for the way we lived.

This is not an unusual story, but my point is that I know the feelings of abandonment, the feelings of "what will become of me", and the feelings of not being loved the way I wanted to be loved. With my extreme sensitivity, I let these feelings go deep into the core of me. The hurt has affected my life in so many ways. For years I have intellectually understood what happened and gone through steps of grieving and forgiveness. Yet, there are times in my life when something quite illusive hurts within me. I cannot adequately describe the feeling, but I know it well. It is whatever fragment is left of the wounded inner child.

Just growing up in a dysfunctional home--and there are many—we carry a wide variety of feelings from wondering whether or not anyone will love us to whether or not we will ever feel safe. I highly recommend two excellent books on the inner child: *Healing the Child Within, by Charles Whitfield, M.D. and on The Family, by John Bradshaw*. There is much healing to be done in our society because of family dysfunctions. It is through the process of healing the inner child that has helped me so much, and it is through my faith in a Divine source that is forever letting me know I am cared for that has enabled me to transform my life. It sometimes takes a lifetime to find the wholeness we seek. However, it is in the journey itself that we find greater meaning in our lives as we meet the challenges of change.

Change is happening all over the world and with great intensity. We can no longer look at our isolated cases of change and deal with them on just an individual basis. I believe it is imperative we also look at how universal change affects us. We need strength and courage to handle the massive changes not only in our own society, but throughout the world. I don't believe we can adequately do this without first healing the past, and for some it has to begin with looking at the wounded child within. We need to embrace this child, perhaps grieve over the difficult times, forgive those who have seemingly hurt us, and finally awaken to what we are here for.

That awakening will help us move out of the wound into a more vibrant and creative life. We will be able to perceive that through it all we have been given tremendous gifts that will help not only ourselves but humanity as a whole. I feel in my heart there is great hope for all of us. As we begin to see our world differently and to see ourselves differently, we will begin a new kind of life built on loving and trusting. Then, we are able to go with change, whatever it might be, and see that it is part of a divine plan. This is when we are able to feel safe in our world. I wrote the following poem as I thought about my own experience with my inner child:

DEAR, SWEET CHILD, COME TO MY BOSOM
FEEL MY HEART AGAINST YOURS.
THIS IS A SAFE HAVEN WHERE YOU CAN
RELEASE YOUR FEARS
AND AWAKEN TO YOUR WORLD OF JOY
AND HAPPINESS.
THIS IS A PLACE WHERE YOU CAN CREATE
THAT WHICH YOU TRULY ARE.

We are the ones best suited to care for our inner child. We have felt the pain and now we must let the past go. It is easier to do this because we now have greater understanding and compassion for ourselves and for mankind, as a whole. We can embrace this precious child, love her dearly, and assure her that she is truly safe. We all need to have a relationship with our inner child. Let her know you love her. Touch her; ask her what she needs so you can transcend the pain you have carried for such a long time. Claiming this part of yourself will allow you to move forward in your life, using your incredible creativity and imagination to bring about loving and satisfying relationships.

CHAPTER SIX
RELATIONSHIPS

If we only knew how important all of our relationships were we would not treat them as though they were burdens or seek only for our own benefit. It is the closest relationships that are the most challenging. These are the ones where we learn our greatest lessons. Every single relationship is about honoring ourselves and honoring another person. Why is it so difficult to do this?

I believe the bottom line is we have not yet learned to really love. . . not ourselves and not each other. It seems reasonable to believe that this is why we are all here on this planet. Love requires much of us, and we fall short because of our human frailties that have caused us to act out of fear rather than love, and because we have not learned to forgive ourselves and to forgive each other. I am not talking about loving someone's hurtful actions, but rather to see beyond that and see the spirit of someone who has not healed the wounds of the past.

This does not mean you should condone hurtful behavior. If you are living with someone who mistreats you, get some help. You need to feel safe and gain a better understanding of what is happening and how you might be participating in the continuance of abusive behavior. As recent as the sixties and seventies we were still denying how we felt. It was a sign of weakness to speak of our wounds. Support groups have given us entry to letting the secrets out. We are now free to feel the pain of the past and to learn to release it, but we need help. The process of opening up all of this new energy allows us to relate to ourselves, and others, in a new and healthier way. It is good news, but it is hard work. It requires us to get to know ourselves in a new way. We no longer need to hide behind our wounds.

Thinking we need to process our emotional pain over and over again keeps us from moving on with our lives. This probably means we still need the pain, although it is an unconscious belief. Ask yourself the question whether or not you need pain in your life to get other needs met, such as love, attention, permission to rest more, or whatever else it might be. Get help, and then get on with creating this new life that can bring about a new sense of wonderment and appreciation for who you are.

For many years, I carried around a lot of stuff from my past. By the time I was in my early fifties, I committed myself to letting go of even more of the hurts and began cleaning up any unfinished business. I talked with my mother who had died, and I made some amends with her. When I was in my late thirties my paternal grandmother told me one of the family secrets. When my father was young she put him in a foster home because she had just divorced his father and was unable to care for him. Although I had forgiven my father a long time ago for abandoning me, I now began to see him as a young boy reaching out for love, and I wept for his pain. I forgave myself for things I wish I had not said or done. I apologized to my first husband for some of the hurts I had caused him. I began to realize that I wasn't responsible for so many other people, but I was certainly responsible for myself. The load gradually got lighter and lighter. Now, in my later years, I'm free from carrying those burdens, and it seems to have made room for more love and understanding to come in.

It is important for me to see how my relationships with my adult children are going and where they can be improved. We cannot take things for granted. We must communicate with our loved ones and seek out the very best relationships possible. If the other person is not willing to cooperate, there will be the right time for that too. Just keep giving out love. For me, writing is much easier than verbalizing. Somehow, when I write I can get down to the heart of things. My children get notes and letters from me, and I can be rather candid with them. I am fortunate that my children know me, whether they want to or not. Of course, everything needs to be used with some discretion. It is not my job to unload my feelings or my burdens on my children. I am not talking about that. I feel it is important that our children see us as individuals with our own feelings and dreams. We are more than just Mom.

Seeking to do our best in all of our relationships gives us much insight into what the divine plan is for us. The people in our lives show us our strengths and our weaknesses that can help us in our self-growth. Because I have moved around a lot, my relationships often changed. This has offered me many opportunities to view life differently. If we stay in the same circle of friends throughout our lives, we close doors to the new. Unless your friends are on their own pathway of self-growth, there is the danger of becoming very limited in what you believe about yourself and the people around you. Life is so rich with diversity. We don't always have to consider another's lifestyle for our own, but let's honor these people for who they are.

I believe close friendships are becoming rare in our busy society. For working mothers, there is very little time left to meet with a trusting friend, but these relationships are extremely important. Maybe it takes weeding out our relationships to see which ones have been nurturing and supportive. I once heard a woman say, "I don't know why I even see Karen anymore. I feel exhausted when I leave." There is something lacking in that relationship. Don't do that to yourself, or to someone else. Our relationships should come from a place of honor, respect, and genuine caring. We all have times when we need to share something with a trusting person. Remember, good friends don't give advice unless they are asked. They just listen.

The marriage relationship is the most challenging of all because that person is a direct reflection of our own inadequacies, our own fears, and our unwillingness to change. We will fight this theory because we have not looked deep enough within ourselves and taken responsibility for those parts of ourselves that we do not want to claim. Women who stay in violent marriages have a tremendous amount of fear about their ability to take care of themselves, and their self-worth is extremely low. Many take the abuse because they feel they don't deserve any better. They do not yet know who they are. I encourage every woman who is presently enduring physical or emotional abuse to leave the home and go for help. Deciding to work on making constructive changes while staying in an abusive relationship can often be used as fuel for more anger. Know you are dealing with a very sick and irrational person.

More and more battered women's programs are now available in most large cities, and there is a battered hotline. Also, Women Helping Women groups are doing wonderful work. Check to see which programs are available in your own city. I bless all women's shelters who give safety to many women as they try to work through some of their issues. I can only have great compassion for these women, as it is difficult for them to break through the illusion that they are victims. In a sense, we are all victims of victims, but through greater compassion for ourselves and a desire to go beyond that victim role, we can free ourselves, but we need to seek out help.

Many young women today wait until they are older to marry. I think this is very wise because it gives them an opportunity to better know who they are and what their needs are. And, I feel they are viewing marriage differently. They want a partnership. They are aware of how their mothers and grandmothers gave so much in the marriage that they didn't know who they really were. Many women thought, "Will I ever have time for me?", but they continued to give their all in pleasing the husband and children, thus denying themselves their own dreams.

I know we can be dedicated wives and mothers and still give ourselves those things that have deep meaning to us. Of course there are times we sacrifice, but there needs to also be the times when others sacrifice for us. We should be able to go off for a two-day outing with friends who nurture us and who allow us to just be ourselves. And, we don't need to feel guilty about it. Many of the young mothers today work full time and maybe that time away seems enough for them. But the fast pace of living today puts a great strain on the family relationships, and other relationships, as well. We must somehow find the balance.

I wonder how many couples take time to sit down and communicate about how they perceive a marriage relationship before they take their vows. First love can be very blind. Rather than true love, we often settle for infatuation or financial security, or both. Then, when we live with a partner, we see their faults and immediately jump in and try to change him. When this happens, there is tremendous danger of ending the relationship without looking at some of the deeper issues. When the daily pressures come in, and they will, open communication is vital. Don't wait until one partner is so stressed out they cannot healthily function in the family system.

A lot of the problems initially begin with one partner, or both, having very low self-worth. It takes a strong sense of self to make a good marriage. Ask yourself the question, "How much do I know about myself?", "Am I in touch with my deep feelings?", "Am I living out of fear?", "Do I feel I deserve a good life?", and "Do I trust myself?" The more you are aware of your own person, the better chance you have to make the marriage or partnership work. Living with someone we thought was "Mr. Right" often shakes us up because we must give up our fantasies of romance being a permanent part of our journey together.

As we move into every day life with our partner, it is natural to experience certain challenges. It is important to share our feelings and to work together in finding workable solutions. If there is a lot of fear surfacing, talk about it. Often, it is simply "change" that requires us to adapt, and it definitely can be a "growing up" time.

We are in the midst of vast change that affects how we view marriage because the rules are changing. With the divorce rate so high, we wonder whether or not we are making an effort to examine our own individual lives to see what is getting in the way of creating a harmonious relationship. It seems to me couples are quick to say they just don't love each other anymore or they have different goals, or whatever.

What happened to commitment? What were your deep intentions when you said, "I do"? What does it take to learn the roles of love, commitment, and trust in making a partnership work? Love alone won't do it. We need to have a foundation of trust; otherwise, we are unable to give and receive the love from each other and to share our innermost feelings. Some of the things I find valuable in seeking a marriage relationship are respect, compromise, sharing and a common set of values. How many of these things do we think about before we establish a living together partnership?

In sharing, there often is a holding back of feelings. Sometimes it is not easy to express what is inside of us, especially that which makes us feel vulnerable, but by doing so we show our intention to work the problems through. This can be a wonderful learning experience if we can stop saying hurtful things about each other. And, I have learned that sometimes I must put some of my own "wants" aside in order to enrich the partnership I am in. We hurt each other tremendously by not communicating our true feelings. Attacking one another is not what I am referring to; that is blaming.

I know that men do not easily get in touch with their feelings, but maybe this is the time to learn. They don't have to be good at it. After all, most men were trained to keep their feelings to themselves, or to completely bury them. So, even mentioning feelings probably is very uncomfortable for them. We, as women, can learn to communicate our feelings in a loving, safe way, thus providing the way to help men do the same. Being skillful at communicating empowers us to say what we are thinking and feeling, and to take some form of action that could help in a difficult situation. If we are taking our self-growth seriously, we will be able to see when life itself calls us to be more. The call may be to have more patience, trust, compassion or faith. It may be in taking on a new perception of the problem or to detach from it enough to settle the emotions.

Let's look at some of the beliefs men and women long ago had as they went into a marriage relationship. Men were taught that they could earn love only by providing, being the head of the family, being in control, and protecting women and children. Many women were taught that they could earn love by being nurturing, cook nice meals, keep the house clean, and being submissive. Now, we are playing by new rules, and it is causing chaos in many relationships because old beliefs are still being carried into our marriages whether we think so or not. Many times we are not even aware of what we are believing.

We really need to talk about what we expect from each other. With relationships in such turmoil, it seems obvious that many of us need to take a good look at our growing-up years to help unravel the misconceptions we now hold about marriage. Ask yourself some of these questions about what went on in your household while you were growing up:

1 - Who made most of the decisions?
2 - Who disciplined the children?

3 - Who was nurturing, if anyone?

4 - What addictive behavior went on, and by whom?

5 - How did your parents treat themselves and each other?

6 - Did your parents openly show affection?

7 - Did they communicate well with each other and with you?

8 - Was there any physical abuse?

As you look at your answers you can probably see beliefs and behaviors that you have carried over into your own intimate relationship.

In the past, long-term relationships survived better because women were well versed in what the rules were and felt we really didn't have too many choices. Today, all kinds of new rules are being written. I believe many women in their fifties, sixties, and seventies still yearn for a closer relationship with their husbands, but it is very difficult adhering to the rules so late. Before expecting someone to follow new rules, we need to work on healing the emotional pain that has kept us from having the kind of marriage we would really like to have. We, older women, begin to hunger for a marriage relationship that goes beyond the needs and beliefs of our earlier years. We want companionship and a sense of caring deeply for the person we are living with. We want openness of our feelings and a sense of being appreciated. And, above all, we want to feel safe.

If years have passed with a strained relationship, it sometimes seems hopeless that it can ever be healed, and we grow bitter with bitter words that only fuel the situation. There is blaming, criticizing, and all manner of creating a worse situation, including no communication at all. It is very, very difficult for someone to communicate if he or she has not developed the skill. A lot of words are not necessary, but honesty, sincerity, and respect are imperative. We must create a safe place to say what we are feeling. No one will open up if they feel they will be under attack. And, if feelings have been held back for a long, long time it will take a special gentleness to help someone say what they feel. I have heard many stories that I feel could have had a better ending.

One of the things I believe gets in the way of honest and loving communication is that we want to be right. There is no right or wrong in most situations. Different people view things differently. We just need to give a little and to let go of all of the resentments that we have built up. Our belittling of each other injures the inner spirit, and our resentment eats away at us like a cancer. Can we learn to cease enacting this harmful behavior to ourselves and to each other? The answer is "yes," if we will work together as partners to create a loving, truthful, and caring way to live together.

Because of the high divorce rate in young couples today, something is glaringly missing. Have we become selfish and controlling? Are we still in a world of illusions concerning what marriage is about? Are we willing to share the deepest part of ourselves that may still hold pain from the past so it doesn't prevent us from having that healthy marriage relationship? I believe there would be much more compassion in marriages if we knew how our partners were feeling versus what they were doing.

As long as we play the game of "Guess why I am acting out this hurtful behavior?", we will continue to put our relationships in jeopardy. We hurt each other tremendously by not communicating to each other our true feelings, and this is difficult for people who are not in touch with their own feelings. People who cannot communicate at the "feeling" level have somehow been taught it is not acceptable or safe to share their feelings.

In earlier years most of us married without knowing much about our spouse's past. Now that so many secrets are out of the closet, some of that has changed. I have met a lot of young married women, and quite a few young married men, who openly speak of the dysfunctions in their earlier home life, and some of the wounds are still raw. I know we hide certain things because we fear we will not be accepted if the other person knows the truth. I hid a lot when I was young.

I think most men would appreciate women being brave enough to share, in a gentle way, some of their fears and concerns. Being open and honest may encourage men to also share. I think men *want* to speak about their feelings, but don't know how. I know from counseling people, and I know from my own personal experiences, that this is a very important issue in helping to make a healthier marriage. We need to share our feelings. We need to say what we mean and not skirt the issues. This can be done in a loving way, but it requires willingness, patience, and practice.

There was a time when I did not feel equipped to say what I was thinking or feeling except in a superficial way. I was fortunate to have a wonderful man in my life at that time who helped me overcome this fear. Seeing me now, people are startled by this comment. Only *we* know our inner most fears and limitations, and we can be good about covering them up. But, it takes energy. Fears and our inability to get in touch with our feelings keep us from being all we are meant to be. And, fears keep us from having healthy relationships. This does not mean we load others down with all of our problems. It only means it is healthy to be who we really are.

Focusing on loving ourselves is one of the greatest ways for us to know ourselves and for us to have loving relationships in our lives. I have a feeling we are going in the right direction by looking at life in a whole new way, knowing it is a lifetime journey and we don't need to do it all now.

After a period of almost twenty years since a divorce, I married again. Having fallen in love with a very dear man, it seemed like a dream come true when he asked me to marry him. It is interesting how we think when we are in a state of bliss. Indeed, this was a "happy ever after" feeling, but I must confess that all of my dreams did not magically unfold. I came out of the bliss state and painfully went through the process of making adjustments in my new life, realizing that Prince Charming was not going to rescue me. I was now vulnerable to feeling some of my old wounds.

When I was alone it was easier to hide from those feelings or to think that I had enough understanding to create the perfect relationship with my husband. Well, it was both humbling and upsetting to realize I still had a long way to go in accepting and loving others just as they are! I found myself in a relationship where the one big belief that was still tucked away in me came out to haunt me. I feel I have now been pruned and honed adequately to accept my husband as he is and to quit trying to change him. I also continue on my pathway of loving and accepting myself more than I ever have before.

My husband is a gentle man, but as with most men, he was unable to share what he was feeling. I think I helped him with that. But, the thing that I was faced with was one wound having laid dormant for so many years while I lived alone after my divorce. I had been studying all of this "good stuff" on how to make a relationship work and found myself resenting things that came about only because I fell back into my old patterns. To know something intellectually and to actually live it out are two different things.

For one thing, the "super woman" in me reappeared, and I literally dropped from exhaustion over the fix-up of my husband's house where I had agreed to live. Then, I realized I married a man whose work seemed the most important thing in his life. Well, I have to tell you I was very angry and in tears a good deal of the time saying, "Maybe I should have stayed single. I feel hurt and unappreciated." Between my husband working full time and falling asleep early in the evening, we have little time together. My inner child is saying, *"I feel abandoned!"* My father abandoned me, and in many ways I felt abandoned in my first marriage. Now, in my senior years, I am working through what I believe to be the final stage of the lingering wound of abandonment.

I share this story because I know many of you have wounds from your past that you are still playing out in your closest relationships. If you're like me, you have not realized what is *really* triggering you off. You think it is something like your partner not pushing the toothpaste out correctly, not paying enough attention to you, or not taking more responsibilty. I wanted to blame my current husband and, even though I tried to see beyond my emotional pain, I dumped a fair amount of blame on him. But, I knew better.

I had studied enough about the inner child to finally see what was happening. I could see how the dynamics played out. It was very clear to me. I came to realize I worked so hard because I still needed a lot of approval from a man. And, I'm saying to myself, "How did that pop up again?" and "How long must I act out harmful behavior to myself in order to get the love I didn't get from my father?" Here is an example of needing to see that I was enough without working myself to a frazzle to prove anything. Well, this was certainly something that needed to be healed once and for all. The idea of changing one's perception of something hit me like a Mack truck. I must have just glossed over this somewhere and thought it was important, but it certainly didn't apply to me! Of course, I was still partly in my world of illusions, but at least I took hold of this concept and worked with it.

I knew I had not made a mistake about marrying this man. Overall, I had come to be in awe of the potential in our relationship and began to respect the mystery of us even coming together to share, to learn, and to love. It is sometimes difficult looking deep within ourselves to see where we all fall short in loving someone, and even more difficult in seeing where we fall short in loving ourselves. I knew I was in the perfect relationship to heal myself of beliefs that continued to keep me from feeling safe in a marriage. It was mostly about my child within who, under certain circumstances, begins to have the old feelings of fear and rejection.

At this point, I had attained great self-worth and self-love, but the old messages were still there waiting to jump out at the first sign of anything remotely like an abandonment issue. I am intrigued how very subtle it can be.

I am expanding on this a bit because I see how very important it is to take responsibility for ourselves and search for those beliefs that we still hold on to that no longer serve us well. Sometimes it takes real soul-searching. At first, I was unable to see the true picture. I just felt the feeling of rejection, and my first impulse was wanting my husband to make it right. In other words, I was blaming him. Working at this level is difficult because we have to be in a place where we are willing to give up the blaming. We must take responsibility for our own feelings and get down to the bottom of what the real issue is.

Look at your own life and see if you can connect with an old wound that keeps you from having a healthy and harmonious relationship with a partner. Somewhere in your past you will discover where you did not get your needs met and your relationship is probably suffering as a result of this. You may go through an experience that is far more serious than mine, and it may be appropriate to end the relationship. But, at least if you have learned where you are vulnerable and see that blaming isn't the answer, you will have learned a great lesson.

If you decide to leave a partner, seek out ways to uncover what the real problem was in your partnership relationships. With more understanding of what has happened and why, you will free yourself to make a better choice next time. Be sure you understand that I am not talking about the woman always being the one to do all the work. If your partner will cooperate in working through his own issues, the whole process will be made easier. But don't count on that happening. Just remember, you are doing this to bring greater wholeness to yourself, and believe it or not, it can be done without your partner changing.

So, if you think you are in the wrong relationship because you are not getting your needs met, think through what I have shared. Perhaps trading in your partner for a new "model" won't be the answer.

Actually, I became so fascinated with what was going on in my own marriage that I was able to be quite objective with what I was seeing. I began to wish I didn't know so much so I could avoid working through this challenge. It is difficult going within and tapping that place where we are vulnerable and where the hurts go very deep. This is the time we need to surrender to something much greater than ourselves and ask for guidance.

I reminded myself that I was not alone. There was the infinite, loving universe helping me through my challenge, so it is best to stop the struggling and just move forward. I didn't have to use a bulldozer. . . I could just take a step at a time. I could sit and be quiet and ask for the Divine wisdom from within. My nature is to get things done NOW, and I am still learning to stop, be quiet, and seek out what I already know to be true at some part of my being.

One thing I knew for sure was I had to put "super woman" to rest. She deserved it, and I had to know that I was good enough without having to prove it in ways that hurt me. Then, I had to watch for that emotional reaction to what I perceived as abandonment because it held a place very deep within me. It pressed all of my emotional buttons.

I must confess that it seemed to have taken me quite a long time to see this so clearly, and I wonder if we aren't all slow learners when it comes to making changes in our lives that we are convinced don't need changing anyway. We're so hung up on trying to change the other person that we don't see what is really happening. I am so much more aware now that I don't think the abandonment issue will ever hit such proportions again because I don't intend to give it that much power. As Caroline Myss says in her incredible book, *Anatomy of the Spirit*, we need to unplug the circuit to a belief that holds us stagnant in our personal growth. It takes a lot of energy to hold a harmful belief like that so long.

Doing this has made a big difference in my relationship with my husband. Instead of harboring over not having much time with him, I am writing this book, and he is very supportive of me as I pursue this endeavor. A yearning had been growing in me for a long time to do this, but I couldn't see the opportunity that appeared before me because I was so upset at not having enough time with my husband. I have grown to love my time alone during the day. And I accept the quiet evenings that refresh me and replenish me.

It suddenly seems so much easier for me to share my feelings with my husband. My husband says he appreciates it when I share with him, and I have learned not to expect him to share anything back. If he does, that is wonderful! I know I have to create a safe place for him to talk of his feelings. I am giving this relationship my all so that both my husband and myself may grow even closer by supporting each other through all our life experiences. This does not mean I give where it becomes hurtful to me. Actually, I am amazed at how my husband finds new ways of giving to me.

Do I deserve a good, healthy relationship? You bet I do, and so do you! You may not be ready to go as deep as I have discussed here, but if you contemplate these ideas, the time will come when you are ready. Begin to think of ways your needs were not met when you were young. Search your own heart regarding what needs to be changed in your life. Something within you knows what you are ready for. Be still and get in touch with your deeper feelings.

In order to grow spiritually, it becomes necessary to peel

away those beliefs that restrict our own growth through anger and resentment. We need to be willing to drop any self-righteousness and to move into a loving and forgiving state. It is so easy to think we are right and they are wrong. Let's remind ourselves to listen to the small voice within so we will be in touch with what our heart is saying.

Whether it is non-acceptance of our partners, or anyone else in our lives, I have learned that it is myself that needs to change. Yes, I know a lot of you will have a hard time with this idea. You will say, "But, you don't understand," and I will recourse, "Oh yes, I do understand because I have used all of those arguments too." Of course, it is difficult seeing the other person's side, but we are called to go beyond finding fault with others, so let's see if we can cooperate in finding a meeting place. The changes we may need to make could be in our perception of a situation or our need for more detachment. Or, it might be tapping into an old belief to see if we need to change that belief. It is possible a situation will call for a separation so couples can have time to think things through.

Our goal should always be about learning to love at a much deeper level than we have ever known before. This does not mean we should condone hurtful behavior. If your belief system has attracted a man who is filled with anger and is taking it out on you, you need to remove yourself from that situation and immediately begin a self-esteem and self-nurturing program.

I wanted to share my experience with you because I see so clearly that we need to look beyond our petty differences and examine our beliefs in order to see where we allow our hurts from the past to affect us in our current relationships. I believe too many relationships suffer because we do not understand where the deeper issues lie. We need to learn to love and accept each other by putting blame aside and by being willing to look at where we are in our own lives and to what extent we have been able to deal with the wounds of the past.

Really look at your day-to-day living to see how you have held on to hurtful events of the past. By doing this and sharing it with your partner, it could make a huge difference in the way he treats you. And, you may be surprised at how willing he is to support you.

I know where I am vulnerable, and I know it is not my husband's job to make me feel safe all the time. I expect him to show understanding and compassion for me while I work through this, but the answer is not in having him work less. He may choose to do that, and I think it would give us both an opportunity to grow even closer, but that is his choice. I see him moving slowly toward that end. We cannot always have what we want when we want it. Many times, when we get it we see we don't want it after all. That is childish behavior. Well, this is just my story. Your story will be different.

Some stories show clearly that the appropriate course of action is to end the relationship. But, don't think that just changing partners is going to make everything perfect. That is the illusion we need to drop. The question is, "Have we learned the lesson?" I have given this example as it pertained to a husband, but this relates to all of our relationships.

For women who are not in a partnership relationship, use this time wisely. Get to know yourself. Nurture yourself and deal with your inner child by forgiving, healing, and moving forward. This will make room for the new and will help prepare you for that special relationship yet to come because you will know who you are!

As we see the many problems that are surfacing with the behavior of children today, it is imperative that we strive to have an open and honest relationship with our children. With so many mothers working today, it is difficult to give the children as much time as I know you would want. It will take sacrificing somewhere because each and every child yearns to be nurtured and loved in a special way.

Whatever time you give them, sit down with them and really hear what they are saying. I remember when my youngest daughter was about eight years old she came to me while I was doing something at the kitchen sink. She spoke to me, and when I began to answer her, she said, "Mommy, I want you to look at me." It made such an impression on me that I never forgot it, and from that time on I tried to be totally "with" my children when they spoke to me. I'm sure there were times when I failed. Children remind us of what's important. They help return us to a too-often lost perspective where we stand today compared to the generations before us.

I heard about one mother who said, "My children give me an opportunity to become a better person by being more patient and understanding. I know by doing this I will have a better chance of getting it back from them." Of course, we dearly love our children, but we do not own them. We are simply guardians of their souls. They are part of the Divine energy and we are, mutually, here to work through our unfinished business in the smallest and the largest experiences we have together.

I am strongly led to bring up the heart wrenching issue of children caught in the middle of a divorce. When I divorced, my children were grown; the youngest eighteen, but there were problems even then. Most young children need two parents living together in order to feel safe and to feel accepted. With younger children, I think it is very, very hard for them to adapt to a divorce situation, especially when they have acquired a stepparent. It is important that parents share a common view on what a child can do and what they are not permitted to do, and follow through on it.

We can say that children are pliable, and that may be true to some extent, but most children are devastated to have one of the parents leave the home. And, in their attempt to have a relationship with both parents, they often feel they are in the middle of a big problem that threatens their stability and puts them in a state of trying not to "rock the boat." I know it is extremely difficult when divorced parents do not get along. But we are talking about the safety, nurturing, and understanding of an extremely large number of young children.

There are many, many questions that children have that are never shared and never answered. I am not suggesting that parents stay in a very bad relationship because of the children. However, I think some marriages could be saved if issues were worked through. Even if the walls of healthy communication have been torn down, it is sometimes possible to rebuild by going for help. The problem is enormous, but if we take responsibility for our own lives, seek out our higher power for some of the answers, and slow down long enough to receive the answers, we will begin to get in touch with ways to heal this mammoth challenge.

Let us remember that we can work through our problems better when we give ourselves "quiet time" and self nurturing. I know many of you think you just don't have time for these things. But, if you set aside fifteen minutes or one-half hour a day for yourself, you will more easily take care of the various tasks before you because you are calm and receptive.

We, as women, are keepers of all of the children, not just our own. In some way, if only by thoughts and prayers, we can assist children who are feeling the emotional pain and confusion that divorces often bring.

It takes a lot of energy to raise a child. Many husbands today are participating more in being there for their children, especially when the mother is working. Whatever the arrangement might be for child care, let it be loving and nurturing. We cannot think that day care centers will take the place of parents.

Our job becomes even greater when our young children are away from us more of the time. It takes a lot of time to give a child love by providing all of the ways in which a child is cared for--laundry, marketing, cooking, dropping them off and picking them up from various activities, caring for them when they are ill, and just plain letting them know we are there for them. It takes time to explain to a child truthful and appropriate answers to all of his or her questions. It takes intuition and skill to track his or her thoughts and feelings. It takes more than most of us are willing, or even capable of giving, to protect a child from some of the harmful stimuli of the world.

By making a concerted effort to work with our children, we will reap the rewards because we are helping to create a better world for them to live in. And, above all, we must allow our children to develop into who they truly are, not a reflection of what we think they should be. Each child is unique with his or her own magnificence. We must work toward guiding them to be all they are meant to be.

It is not just when the children are young that we need to think about our relationship with them. I find that my relationships with my three adult children, and with my grandchildren, need improving on a regular basis. For a number of years my son and I would ask each other what we needed from one another in working toward an even better relationship. Somewhere along the line that got lost, but I am reminded that this is a good thing to do because sometimes we do not ask for what we need. We assume the other person just wasn't able to give anymore or doesn't care, but that is not necessarily true.

Those of us who are brave enough and willing enough to give even more of ourselves in a relationship will reap the rewards. Seeking out the very best in our relationships is part of the spiritual journey. There doesn't have to be an element of fairness in this. . . "I will do this if you do this." It needs to be because we want to give. However, if you give until you feel totally depleted, that could be another issue altogether. We have the capacity to give so much and let it be of our love and devotion and not so much with material things.

Friendship relationships are so important. Women need other women with whom to share their joys and their sorrows. Part of our journey to wholeness is getting support from our women friends who often have struggled with some of the same challenges. The bond of friendship seems to be falling by the wayside as we work more hours, commute long distances, and isolate ourselves by watching television and using our computers.

I don't think we need lots of friends, but choose them wisely and use them for mutual growth. Let them come from a place of honor, respect, and genuine caring. With so many women working today it may seem difficult to give the time to nurture these friendships. Actually, I don't think they require a lot of time, but the relationship must hold in it a feeling that your friends will love and support you, no matter what. We all have times when we need to share something with a trusting person. This helps us to get a new perspective on our lives.

I have found the issue of control most interesting in viewing relationships, and I confess I continue to work on releasing my own need to step in and try to make things happen. For me, it has been helpful to understand why I have felt the need to do this. I understand that children growing up in very dysfunctional homes learn early to control. Women in particular, try to control the so-called uncontrollable parts of their lives during their early years. There seems to be a need to try to make things better by coming up with new solutions to the problem. This is not bad in itself, but it is usually accompanied by fear.

My mother was a master at trying to keep things under control in our home with my dad's drinking and inability to hold down a job. Children often end up automatically thinking that is the only way to handle situations. I don't believe this is bad, but rather something that was necessary at the time. Certainly, we aren't intentionally hurting someone, especially ourselves, but somewhere along the line controlling became a survival tactic and we hung on to it. As we grow in our own awareness of what works for us in life, it is good to reassess how we react to challenging situations, or any situation, for that matter.

I, personally, came to a place where I found it too exhausting to believe I must come up with a proper solution for everything in my life, including trying to change my husband and the lives of my children. Don't confuse control with being efficient and creative and having the ability to bring new ideas to the attention of others. I am talking about the need to make sure others know of *my* way of solving a problem or showing in some way that I am not pleased with the way someone is handling his or her situation.

We cannot, and really should not protect our grown children from making their mistakes. Sometimes it is in the solving of a terribly painful challenge that they learn the best lessons. This is a very delicate issue, but as we allow love to take us by the hand and bring us to greater understanding and compassion, we will naturally let the control go. We have enough to do to just control our own lives.

I find there is a very fine line of discernment in everything we try to do for our children. We, as women, feel a real need to raise our children the very best we know how. We need to teach our children that there are certain boundaries where things are acceptable or unacceptable. This is for their own safety and for society as a whole. Many times parents are not capable of doing this and many children grow up not setting boundaries for themselves, thus being used, abused, and often feeling hostile. This results in a tremendous amount of pent-up anger held inside. Often this anger is displaced, thus hurting those who are closest to them, and sometimes themselves. So, there is a need for healthy control in the earlier years of a child. But, as parents, we must learn to draw our own line of discernment.

Certainly, as our children grow older we should be able to release more control. This is called letting go. Our children will make some mistakes, but many times it is the mistakes that help them learn. The goal is not to be the perfect parent, perfect wife, or perfect friend, but as we continue our spiritual journey we will be aware of new ways in which to deal with our relationships. The way we handle our own lives will be what our children will remember and not what we tell them to do.

Many issues that come up between partners are control issues. Some people call them power issues. I think they are one and the same. One doesn't necessarily control by words, but by actions. It takes a lot of energy trying to control others. Don't do that to yourself. And it takes a great deal of patience to maintain truly loving relationships.

I know we all have human frailties, and these ideas are not meant to make you feel inadequate or that you must strive to be perfect. We all have different challenges in our lives, and not everyone is equipped to handle things in what might seem to be the most loving way. I believe we are doing the best we can for the understanding we have at this time. But, let us stay open to learning even better ways of communicating with our loved ones. All relationships are important, but the most precious relationship is the one you are building with yourself. Let's get to know and love ourselves better and be willing to look with the eyes of love in dealing with the people in our lives.

CHAPTER SEVEN
CARING FOR OUR BODIES

Our bodies are such miracles, but how often do we give thanks for what they do for us? How often do we nurture them, lovingly touch them? It both fascinates and frightens me how we mistreat our bodies. In the hectic pace of today's living we don't take the precious moments we need to stop and feel what is happening in our bodies. We just charge on and then collapse at the end of the day. It sounds familiar to me. . . I've done it.

At the age of about forty-nine I began to reprogram my mind about my beliefs and about my body. Oh, I had taken care of myself quite well over the years, eating fairly well, exercising, and I was blessed with a very optimistic nature. However, I realized that I had to seriously begin a day-to-day awareness of what I was doing to my body. I became aware of the tense way I approached my daily tasks, often ending up with back pain. I had become stronger in my belief about having the power within me to change my circumstances.

The idea that I was a co-creator with my Divine source completely turned things around for me. I knew I had to learn to relax my muscles. Since those were the days I was acting out my "super woman" role, I found it a real challenge to slow down enough to quit hurting myself. I began to find my "quiet times" extremely powerful, and I was ready to answer the call to change. If you're like I was, you probably are not even aware of the abusive way you sometimes treat your body.

It is a powerful feeling to believe you are capable of making mammoth changes in how you live your life. This is not about taking a class in how to force your mind to do something. This is about "internal power." I was perfectly aware that it was my Divine source empowering me to act more lovingly to myself.

I have come to see that the possibilities for being all I am meant to be are limitless. Of course, it meant taking responsibility for my life, and that included giving up totally relying on others to promote good health habits for me. I began to get more serious about participating in creating good health for myself. I chose healthier foods, and I began a program of exercise. I began to see my body as such a wonderful gift. I thought about each part of my body, and I blessed it. I allowed these new thoughts to permeate my being, and soon I was able to have a whole new feeling about my entire body. . . what a wonder it was, and how I must always remember to treat it lovingly.

My "quiet times" reinforced my need to really be good to myself. Sometimes I would slide back into my old ways of wanting to run the whole show. After exhausting myself, I would realize what I was doing, and get back to honoring my inner wisdom. When we are able to establish a new belief about the body and our ability to change, we automatically think in new ways that result in being much kinder with ourselves. We eat healthier food, get more rest, exercise, and nurture ourselves. We don't struggle with it because eventually the mind is programmed, and the body is loving the way we are treating it.

Our Western culture does not teach us to value our bodies. We are over worked, overfed, and lack the education of how our bodies work and how they crave for love and affection. It seems we need to examine and change some of the beliefs and assumptions we have been taught by our culture.

In her book, *Women's Bodies, Women's Wisdom*, Dr. Christiane Northrup boldly writes, "We're not even close to understanding how our bodily systems interact with each other, let alone how they interact with other people. . . . We cannot hope to reclaim our bodily wisdom and inherent ability to create health without first understanding the influence of our society on how we think about and care for our bodies." Dr. Northrup claims that we are out of touch with how we feel because the rules were established long ago that women have inferior bodies and that they are constantly in need of fixing. She encourages women to go beyond the physiological part of the body by learning to listen to the wisdom of their bodies.

How women feel about their bodies still reveals a belief system that says our female hormones, organs, and body parts do not support us, thus greeting hormone replacement therapy, and often unnecessary surgeries, as welcome solutions for many of our discomforts. There seems to be a belief that we all will experience pain and discomfort because the Creator made a mistake. I don't think so!

There is no one to blame. We are merely evolving, and it is time that we wake up and view our bodies differently. Our bodies will continue to suffer in some way as long as we do not honor them. We are trained to look outside of ourselves for help, totally discounting that we have the innate wisdom to help ourselves in so many ways. Join me in traveling this more empowered pathway by committing yourself to a new way of promoting better health for yourself.

In 1996 I had the shock of my life. I had a mammogram that showed no breast abnormalities. I should have felt relieved. But several weeks prior to the exam I had an incredible sensation that something was wrong with my left breast. When I told the radiologist this, he showed me my X rays and said he was sure everything was okay. But, I couldn't let it go and asked for some other way of checking for a possible lump. He agreed to ultrasound, and there it was, barely detectable. Again, the radiologist said he thought it certainly would test benign, but it didn't. I was faced with the fact that I had cancer.

I was fortunate to have found the cancer so early in its development, but it was found because I spoke up and because I had an intuitive sense that something was wrong. We must know by now that doctors are limited in their ability to treat our illnesses and diseases. We must take on certain responsibilities if we want to live a more healthful life and, in my opinion, this means we need to develop our own intuition.

We are at a totally new place regarding how our bodies function and the power we have within us to help in their healing. Ideally, we need to develop our intuition in a way where we can sense what is happening before serious symptoms develop. I encourage you to at least begin by giving yourself the gift of "quiet time" that will enable you to tap into the messages you need to hear.

Having cancer taught me what I thought I already

believed, but experience is the real teacher. Yes, I felt some fear when I was told I had cancer. I actually shook inside, but some part of me knew I was going to be all right. I tried to stay calm, getting all the information from the surgeon, and then doing the most powerful thing we can do and that was to ask for Divine guidance in making my decisions. I did not rush into getting surgery. I needed the time to get a sense about what was in my best interest. I cried, and I prayed. I *did* end up with a lumpectomy and the removal of a few lymph nodes, two of which were cancerous. And I had radiation. When the crisis is about *us* it is so easy to panic and do everything the doctor feels is right for us, forgetting to seek out answers from within.

I made the decision to have surgery and radiation, but I knew I had to take a good look at my day-to-day living patterns. *What did I need to change? What was creating stress in my life? I had been so tired, what was causing that tiredness?* My goal was to create a real "aliveness" in me. I knew how I felt inside, and the feelings I had masked in the past were staring at me now. They revealed themselves during my convalescence, and I knew without a doubt that the first thing I needed to do was to slow down and be much kinder to myself.

I entered my sacred place morning, noon, and night and felt the healing power of the Divine. In the past I knew there were times when my body called out for help, and I did not give it to myself. But now I have learned to recognize those feelings before they go too far. I remember how tired I was during the two years prior to discovering cancer. I thought about breasts representing nurturing and sustenance. As I reflected on my tendency to nurture others, I realized I gave-gave-gave.

I began to see so clearly that we, as women, are not meant to give until the well is dry. I started a wonderful self-nurturing program for myself where the tears flowed in recognition of what I so desperately needed. This doesn't mean I caused my disease. It only means that it was time to look at ways in which I could express much more love for my body, mind, and spirit. I see this as an important part of preventative medicine.

After surgery, I found it a great relief to just rest and be good to myself. I remember thinking, "It is okay to rest now that I have a reason to stop my frantic actions." This thinking greatly alarmed me! Do I need cancer in order to slow me down? These thoughts stayed with me, and my "quiet times" helped me to reinforce my need to let go of things that really were not that important and just take care of myself. By the time I had radiation, I felt rested and was comfortable with my decision to have it. I made declarations of healing as the radiation went into my body. I knew a greater power was working in me. I was so at peace with myself. Through all of this, I remembered to bless my body much more often. I began to catch myself as I crossed the line of comfort in my daily activities.

I am still learning to give myself more time for something that is truly special to me. I have learned to take very good care of myself most of the time. I add "most of the time" because I know the "old me" comes creeping out from time to time, and I have to just bless her and remind her how important it is to treat her body lovingly. I am now cancer free, and I believe I will stay that way. This is an example of how a challenge can be turned into an opportunity; an opportunity to establish greater faith and a better understanding of who we are and what we need. I cannot imagine going through this type of experience without having faith that something far greater than myself was with me, guiding me during surgery and radiation, as well as during my convalescence.

Through my own breast cancer experience I learned a lot about my body. I had to research, I had to rely on my own inner wisdom, and I had to go against some of what the medical profession was telling me. I came to believe I had been given too much estrogen for my body since the biopsy showed me to be estrogen receptive, meaning I was high risk for cancer because my body acted adversely to the estrogen I was taking. So, I immediately went off of any kind of estrogen. Of course, I entered menopause because my estrogen level plummeted. The hot flashes felt as though someone had lit a match to me.

My doctors could not come up with any solution to relieve these symptoms without estrogen nor did they think to tell me to gradually reduce the estrogen. But, my acupressure practitioner told me about a sympathetic doctor who worked almost exclusively with women experiencing cancer, and he assisted me in a program of using natural progesterone. Even though my uterus and ovaries had been removed years earlier, Dr. Lee claimed the progesterone would help me not only avoid menopausal symptoms, but would reduce chances of bone loss, and that it was safe to take. My hot flashes went away within a week, and as recent as this writing I am holding my own concerning bone loss.

I will never forget what this compassionate doctor did for me. I began to read page after page of medical research, some from Dr. Lee's book, *What Your Doctor May Not Tell You About Menopause,* and some I found on my own. I began to feel there were many things women had not been told about the use of estrogen, and about issues such as natural progesterone. I got the feeling that I was becoming somewhat empowered to make a difference in how I looked at my body, how I could find help, and how I could share my own experiences with other women. I also want to let you know that Dr. Lee has another book coming out in early 2002, *What Your Doctor May Not Tell You About Breast Cancer.*

The other day I was tremendously relieved to hear a gynecologist on television give warnings about using unopposed estrogen (not balanced with natural progesterone). Breast and uterine cancer are on the rise. We need to encourage women to get better educated and to become more aware of what they are putting into their bodies. This applies to all medications we might need to take. Educating ourselves and asking more questions empowers us to make better decisions.

Many of you may be able to take estrogen. However, I do hold a great concern over the way pharmaceutical companies are pushing estrogen as though it is the answer for all of women's physical and emotional problems, and most doctors seem to concur. Dr. Christiane Northrup has questioned what the medical profession as a whole has been telling us. Her feeling is that estrogen may be necessary for some women, but she feels it should be very carefully monitored and should contain natural progesterone.

Most pharmaceutical estrogens have progestin, which is toxic to the body. For those of you who are not familiar with the various kinds of estrogen, Estriol is by far the safest estrogen to use. However, pharmaceutical companies do not use it. I have been able to find it through a lot of calling and searching for pharmacies who make up special compounds. The same doctor who alerted me to natural progesterone advised me it was safe to use a limited amount of estriol estrogen to relieve irritation of the vaginal lining thus avoiding infections. Estrogen certainly has a place in our lives, but how much and what kind are vital issues.

I strongly believe estrogen is not going to be the magic pill that will cure women's menstrual challenges, offer them a safe treatment when they have had their uteruses and ovaries removed, and bring them relief during the aging process. I am not questioning whether or not a woman feels better while on estrogen. I'm sure I received some benefits while taking it, but my long-term use of estrogen without proper balancing of progesterone brings me to think there was a far better way to treat me. The long term use of estrogen has become so questionable, even within some of the medical profession, that I think women ought to ask a lot of questions before taking it and staying on it for an extended amount of time.

The main reason I am making such a point of estrogen is that, whatever the medication might be that a doctor prescribes, we need to ask some questions. This is how we empower ourselves to make decisions. Don't let the doctor alone make the decision for you. It is your body, and extremely precious to you. We so lack in understanding how our bodies function, but we can change that. Most of us don't even know where many of our organs are located. We have left everything up to the doctors. Now, we must take responsibility for ourselves, get in touch with our bodies, and take part in making decisions regarding our overall health. Other people, including professionals, are not always right.

I continue to research those things that give me cause to see if there are safer ways to keep me healthy. We have to live out the choices we have made in the past when we were not as aware. But, I do know there is great hope for all women to be able to assist in treating their own bodies with loving care, and with medications and treatments that we feel good about. This not only helps you, but your families as well. I hope each of you will consider joining me in this important endeavor. As you take the first step in asking questions, you will feel so good about your ability to speak up that you will continue to educate yourself. And, during your "quiet times", you will ask your inner wisdom for help.

Personal experiences that I share in this book are meant to make you think. As we begin to make some better health choices for ourselves, we can live life in a whole different way. Then we need to pass this new information on to other women, especially our daughters, to begin early to value their bodies enough to ask doctors questions about why they may not want to take a certain medication or have a particular surgery. This leaves room for discussion. In the past, many women have said, "Just cut it out so I don't have to deal with it." If we do that, we are not in touch with our bodily wisdom, and we may risk having problems later. From my own experience, my final decision was to have surgery, but I got all the facts first.

I know this is new to a lot of you, but that is why I am writing this book as a lay person who has experienced enough to know we are worth having the best possible care, and that it is imperative that we participate in healing whatever we are presently experiencing whether it be physical, emotional, or spiritual. The first step is to get in touch with what your body is telling you.

Don't misunderstand me, I am not angry with the doctors.

We are the ones who have given them so much power. We must begin to take back the power that, ultimately, will allow us to work with our doctors. As we become more active in our own health decisions and continue to work on placing greater value on our intuitive wisdom, life itself will help us get the information we need. Learning to speak up for ourselves will not only help us to take care of our bodies, but it will give us a sense of empowerment that will assist us in every area of our lives.

I cringe when I think about what society, as a whole, believes about women's menstrual cycle. Over the years there has been a lot of distortions on just how miraculous and beautiful this cycle of life is. The menstrual cycle is actually part of our inner guidance system. It can be a very meaningful and creative time for women, but we have been taught that having our periods is a curse; a terrible thing to tell a young girl. Most girls are not emotionally prepared to grasp what their female sexuality is all about. I know I wasn't! I would think that understanding how our own uterus, fallopian tubes, ovaries and menstrual cycle work would help immensely. Maybe some of this is taught today. If not, we certainly need to educate young girls of the "miracle" that is involved here.

Many women have been brainwashed to think their menstrual cycle is a time they should dread. And, often there is shame and even humiliation attached to this natural womanly function. It is time to change all of that. It is true that as we approach the premenstrual time we go more inward, and we feel our emotional pain. But this is good, except we have been taught to guard against any feeling of our inner emotions. Many women are more in touch with their own creativity at this time, so try to write down some of the feelings you have during this cycle. Later you can put some of them into action and share these experiences with others. It is obvious we need to pass on some new information regarding menstruation.

The premenstrual syndrome comes when we do not honor our need to rest and to be gentle with ourselves. Our society is so action prone that we are often not in touch with our need for rest and replenishment. Can we learn to give ourselves permission to retreat from some of our duties at this time and gain the wisdom that is trying to break through? It would be wonderful to think that women could actually set aside time just to nurture themselves and have some "quiet time" during their menstrual cycle. When we feel emotional about something, it is something we need to lovingly take a look at.

Men need to understand this too and allow us to move through this cycle in a way that is beneficial for us. If men could become more aware of woman's deep need to be understood and nurtured, I am sure many would give their wives some pampering at this time of the month. When we value ourselves enough, we will feel good about asking our husbands for more nurturing at this important time. As women, we need to change our own thinking on this issue and begin to retrain our daughters to better understand their menstrual cycles. They can, then, view this special time of the month as something sacred and begin to move through the experience with greater ease.

Let's celebrate being "woman" by learning to appreciate our wonderful bodies and their ability to create life. If we will flow with the natural cycles and nurture ourselves in some very special ways, we will find meaning for all the phases of life. We have much to learn about our bodies.

Caroline Myss, in her book, *Anatomy of the Spirit*, says that cramps and PMS are classic indications that a woman is in some kind of conflict with being a woman. My reply to that comment is, she probably is because she has been brought up to think her body is betraying her in some way, not understanding the truth about what the menstrual cycle is all about. Take special care in giving your body lots of love and attention as you enter your menstrual cycle. This is a beautiful act of loving yourself.

More and more chronic illnesses are rising to the surface in women today, such as pelvic pain, chronic fatigue syndrome, and fibromyalgia. Let's refrain from thinking these problems are just part of being a woman and having a disease that we have no control over. Dr. Northrup found that her women patients experiencing these particular diseases were prone to taking on far too much in their day-to-day responsibilities.

Some of us have been trained to do it all. I fall into this group. When I was acting out my "super woman" role, I could do just about anything and do it well. My mentality was, "If you want something done right, you have to do it yourself." I also felt guilty if I didn't respond to other people's requests. I began to have many symptoms of fibromyalgia. I learned about a product called magnesium malate through a jin shin jyutsu acupressure practitioner. (There is a wonderful little book out, *The Touch of Healing*, by Alice Burmeister which gives ways in which we can use the ancient art of jin shin jyutsu on ourselves.) I began to take the magnesium malate and continued my acupressure treatments, but I knew I also needed to take a serious look at my life to see how I was taking on more than my body wanted or needed. I began to let go of my need to make things perfect, and I let loose of my need to make things right for the loved ones in my life, as though I even knew what was right for them. And I began to give myself even more of that precious gift of "quiet time." Two years later I was free of any of the symptoms of this illness.

I'm still prone to pushing beyond my means, but I can catch myself now and remind myself that doing this is not being loving to myself. I don't want to lose that part of me that is thoughtful and loving, but I have learned that I have to create certain boundaries for myself regarding how much I do in order to prevent new symptoms from arising that could create illness. At first it was difficult saying "no", but I have found a very loving way of just saying, "I'm sorry I can't; I need to take care of myself." And, amazingly so, I rarely get those kinds of requests anymore. A leap in consciousness can change how people view you and what they expect from you. Here is the classic example of how our belief system can actually cause physical harm to our bodies.

We will not change the very core of us, nor should we, but we can alter our behavior to make room for a healthier life for ourselves. I most firmly believe there is a correlation between our daily living patterns and some of our discomforts and illnesses. It is not easy changing lifelong patterns, but I believe this is part of the process of healing. We have the power within us to educate ourselves more fully about what will help us heal physically, emotionally, and spiritually. You will find that the education you give yourself will empower you to really make a difference in your total health. We owe it to ourselves, and we owe it to the women who follow us, to speak up for ourselves and to question the authorities about issues that concern our mental, emotional, and physical well-being.

There are many mental and physical exercises one can do

to elicit relaxation responses that help boost the immune system and overcome chronic pain, as well as other stress-related illnesses. There is so much written on the mind/body connection. A book I highly recommend is *Minding the Body, Mending the Mind* by Dr. Joan Borysenko. In her book she points out the demanding process of changing attitudes and ways of living. Dr. Borysenko has become well received by many of her colleagues as she has embraced new and controversial ways of healing.

Joan was moved to enter this somewhat questionable way of treating patients early in her career when she experienced several critical illnesses. Not finding solutions with the routine treatments of the medical profession, she began to research illnesses by going beyond symptoms and reaching for the underlying causes. She came to understand her own body and its symptoms were part of her inner guidance, and that she could tap this part of herself that truly knew the deep psychological and spiritual reasons why she was experiencing these illnesses.

Joan's messages have touched me deeply in a way that transcends society's outlook on our physical and emotional well-being. She states, "If we are willing to give up our stories of fear and gaze with new eyes into the face of love, perhaps someday we will find a new meaning in our suffering." I know there is a Divine purpose for both physical and emotional suffering. I am sure that part of it is to learn from it and to transcend the pain. Stories I have read about women who have been able to transform their pain into wisdom, insight, and compassion tear at my heart. I pray that I might find this kind of faith and be willing to let go of fear along with all of the meaningless ways in which I sometimes live my life.

Certainly, these women have touched the Divine.

I love what Kahlil Gibran wrote in his treasured book, *The Prophet* :

> *"Your pain is the breaking of the shell that*
> *encloses your understanding.*
> *Even as the stone of the fruit must break,*
> *that its heart may stand in the sun, so*
> *must you know pain.*
> *And could you keep your heart in wonder at*
> *the daily miracles of your life, your pain*
> *would not seem less wondrous than your joy;*
> *And you would accept the seasons of your heart,*
> *even as you have always accepted the seasons*
> *that pass over your fields.*
> *And you would watch with serenity through the*
> *winters of your grief."*

There is so much evidence today showing that meditation and other spiritual practices definitely assist us in healing our lives. While we all will have our time of suffering, let's not suffer needlessly. Begin to tap your inner wisdom for ways to live your life in a way that lessens the stresses. Recognize your physical symptoms early so you can heal yourself through receiving insights into their causes. There are no miracle cures out there. *We* are the ones who have the power to assist in healing our bodies in so many ways if we will start early with preventive measures, or at least when the symptoms first appear. But, many women are not in touch with their bodies enough to detect early symptoms and they end up just hoping they don't contract certain illnesses or diseases.

Regardless of our present physical challenges, let us not

lose hope in the compassion of the Divine. Within the hope is the ability to renew and re-create. It comes when we lift ourselves out of our old ways of thinking and see life from a higher perspective. There is value in getting an annual physical, and there is value in using medication or having surgery, but let's also begin also to believe in the miracles that become our reality as we touch our deeper selves. It is not likely that we will prevent all illnesses from entering our bodies, but we can reduce the risk of many diseases by taking good care of ourselves.

I am reading more and more about some doctors who are going beyond the scientific means of healing to see that faith, belief, and imagination can actually unlock the mysteries of why we get ill. Many doctors are now suggesting some of the alternative methods of healing. We are becoming awakened to doctors' limitations, and that is good. In some ways, I think they are relieved that they have been removed from the pedestal of being the Almighty.

Let's stay open to all possibilities as we go beyond what we have believed in the past. Hold on to your faith by looking at life through a child's eyes. Know that you will be given what you need as you seek a higher way of looking at life.

"Ask and it shall be given you;
Seek, and you shall find;
Knock, and it shall be opened to you.

For whoever asks, receives;
And he who seeks, finds;
And to him who knocks, the door is opened."
- —Jesus, Matthew 7:7,8

Certainly, we are not totally responsible for our body's state of health. We are merely beginning to see how our own participation in healing our bodies is essential. This is a gift we give to ourselves. Illnesses may come that we have no control over. Just do your best to stay tuned into your bodily wisdom and begin to perceive the events in your life in a new way.

Some religions believe suffering allows us to drop our masks and reveal our true selves. I am inclined to agree with that. If this is so, I wonder if our wounds don't contain the seeds of something quite extraordinary that can bring us to a state of greater wisdom, compassion, creativity, and love. Maybe that is because our defenses are down during the time of suffering, and we are open to new possibilities for understanding at a deeper level.

It is obvious that we are in need of the spiritual knowledge that unlocks many of the secrets of healing. More and more we are accepting the fact that we have power to help change the state of our health. Until we have educated ourselves and learned to trust our own intuitive powers, we need doctors to perform their duties according to what science has discovered.

I know it may seem overwhelming even to think about taking charge of your own body. To begin with, it could be helpful to see a holistic doctor or practitioner. They have an abundance of information on alternative ways of healing such as meditation, acupuncture, acupressure, exercise, massage, and nutrition. Among these, meditation will help you the most to develop your intuition. Accessing the intuition is extremely valuable and you are the only one who can tap into that sacred place within.

I am not saying that we have the power to cure all of our illnesses. There are times when illness comes and we have done a lot of wonderful things for ourselves. However, to heal does not necessarily mean to cure. Through spiritual means, we can be healed, but a disease may not be cured. There is a distinction to be made here. By changing some of our negative patterns, we can heal our lives in many ways, and I know that *some* illnesses do leave our bodies as we come to greater spiritual wholeness. Through spiritual meditation we can receive a transformation that renews us in some unexplainable way. There simply are some things in life that the human mind cannot perceive, but they become truth for us, and they are born out of faith.

Again, I refer to Dr. Northrup who, along with several other women doctors, opened Woman to Woman Clinic in Yarmouth, Maine, a number of years ago. These doctors address the various health concerns of women. Their approach empowers women to participate in the healing of mind, body, and spirit. Dr. Northrup points out that thoughts, emotions, and the brain communicate directly with our immune, nervous, and endocrine systems as well as with the organs in our bodies. Our concept of how our thought processes and emotions affect our body really needs to be expanded. We used to think of the mind as part of the brain, but now we are told it exists in every cell of our bodies. I don't know about you, but I find this very fascinating. This says that we are much more than we think we are.

In Dr. Northrup's book she states, "Only by living through a serious health problem did I become understanding of what other women with health and life problems are experiencing." Her love, her insights, and her great compassion for women have helped thousands of women take a new look at how they can participate in their own healing. Dr. Northrup's work has crept into many homes via the television and with her book, *Women's Bodies, Women's Wisdom*. I highly recommend that you have your own copy of this book so you can be more aware of the thinking for the new woman of today, and most certainly of the future.

Today there is such a busyness in our culture; we have lost something precious. We don't take time to rest and just enjoy the quietness of even a few hours. There seems to be a belief that doing something all of the time is better than resting, and that we will all be terribly bored if we refrain from work one day a week that I remember well while growing up. It was Sunday, a time to worship, a time to be with family, and a time to rest. Today, with both husband and wife working and all the various activities children participate in, we have lost our ability to just rest and recuperate. We wait until we are sick and then complain because it takes so long to recover. We want a magic pill or some kind of a quick fix so we can go back to that fast pace of living again. We all need some "quiet time", that precious time when we just do nothing! This is when true wisdom comes in. This is when answers to our problems are revealed to us.

Wayne Muller writes in his book, *Sabbath, Restoring the Sacred Rhythm of Rest*: "Successful life has become a violent enterprise. We make war on our own bodies, pushing them beyond their limits; war on our children because we cannot find enough time to be with them when they are hurt and afraid; war on our spirits because we are too preoccupied to listen to the quiet voices that seek to nourish and refresh us." These are thoughts to be taken seriously. I realize many of you have been able to find a proper balance in your lives and that is wonderful. I think most women want to have the "quiet time" but are overwhelmed by work and responsibilities. Some of us have been able to get massages and other treatments to help revitalize our bodies, but many cannot afford them. Proper nutrition is important, but our busy lives have us eating too many frozen dinners and fast foods. Our bodies are not machines; they are living beings and they need our loving care. Covering up our symptoms with external temporary fixes prevents us from healing the parts of our lives that desperately need attention and change. Our bodies sometimes scream to be heard, but do we hear them? Ignoring what your body is trying to tell you more often than not will create some form of illness or disease.

As we continue to learn to love our bodies and to get in touch with what they are telling us, we improve the quality of our lives tremendously. I believe each of you wants maximum health for yourself. Let's not leave it to chance. Just take a moment each day to hold yourself and remind yourself of how precious you are, and that you deserve good health.

CHAPTER EIGHT
OPENING OUR HEARTS TO MEN

As a result of much soul-searching during the process of writing this book, I decided to give the subject of our relationships with men a full chapter. As I begin, I am not even sure how I will fill these pages, but something in my heart is leading me to this place.

Many women have forgotten, in the modern emphasis on a career and economic independence, that woman has a role to play toward man which is inherent in her nature. This role is beyond sharing of intellectual interest, cooking for him, or the many other things that "woman" does in the home. It is not becoming the mother of his children nor being his sexual partner. But, over and beyond all of these other roles, woman needs to nurture man so that he will get in touch with his inner self.

The history of man has taught him to fight and conquer, to provide for his family, and in many ways to "own" his children and wife. Yet, I believe deep within man is an incredible need to have love and support from his "woman" in order that he might fulfill his creative urges and inspirations. He really needs to be believed in. I have given great thought about my own impatience with men and about some deep hurts that I have blamed men for. At times I am torn between what may not yet be healed within me and what is revealed to me through my inner wisdom.

My innermost feelings tell me that men have been greatly misunderstood, and I have tried to see beyond the apparent actions of some men toward me, their wives, and other women. Even with my own feelings of being used and misunderstood at times, I cannot help but see that many men lack the ability to nurture. Perhaps we women have misinterpreted their intentions as being distant and uncaring when, indeed, they lack the skill to show they truly care.

Through much contemplation and forgiveness, I stand here today having a whole new perception of man's own painful journey. I accept responsibility for my own feelings and for where I am in my life compared to even ten or twenty years ago. I see there really is no one to blame. We can perceive things in a different way now, or we can continue to feel victimized.

In my opinion, woman has been chosen to help heal the wounds of men everywhere. I know some of this may not only sound strange, but to some, outrageous. However, we need only to look at how the patriarchal system has placed man at an exalted place. And this belief is crumbling before our very eyes as women move into higher positions in business, in politics, and in the church. Certainly, man also has his natural role and far too many men stray from it. Part of their role is to seek advice from women when she has developed her inner wisdom and as she seeks to support man in his attempt to grow and change. At present, the situation looks rather bleak.

I feel this is the time for both men and women to look at themselves in a new way and to make the changes that will heal some of the misconceived ideas of what the roles of men and women are today. I personally believe man desperately needs certain feminine qualities in order for him to find himself. And, unless he has those in himself, he must seek out woman for help. Obviously men *do* have some feminine qualities, but they are guarded so carefully that most men do not claim them.

It is ludicrous to blame men today for the consciousness of men from years past. Yes, we must continue to make our voices heard and to move forward empowered by our natural female attributes of compassion, cooperation, tolerance, intuition, and nurturance. Many of these qualities have been negated throughout the years and, as a result, have promoted lack of sympathy, a need for external power, and a concentration on the intellect to the point where the heart, in many women, has been suppressed. Perhaps we have needed to go off course for a period of time. But today I see the need to return to the more loving approach in dealing with the men who, at times, put us down in subtle ways and not-so-subtle ways. Let us not return any form of abusiveness to men.

Certainly, there are situations where we definitely need to distance ourselves from men who continue to physically and emotionally abuse us. And, if the men in our lives make jest of our efforts and choose not to cooperate in healing our differences, we have fulfilled our part and they must find their way without us. As we continue to become conscious of our internal power and how to use it, we will find our right place in the world, and it will include using our compassion to help men. As this takes place, I feel many men will respond in a new and positive way that will assist in healing many,, many relationships.

There are few women that I meet who do not have

complaints about their husbands such as not being open, not sharing, boring, distant, weak, and insensitive. Or, they feel men want to work all the time or watch too much television, or whatever. I can only say, from my own experience, we must let go of trying to change the men. We need to work on our own lives to see where we, ourselves, need to change even though it may only be in our perception of a situation.

I am convinced that many men are in great emotional pain, and they may not even realize it because they are so used to hiding their feelings. And, I know many women are in great emotional pain and will find it difficult to use the approach I speak of. My message to you is to concentrate first on yourself until you are healed enough to assist your partner in finding himself through a new kind of power.

Many of today's men are products of a long line of men who learned from the generations that went before them to own, to control, to abuse, to be insensitive, to feel superior, and to be distant, which resulted in them being unable to reach women at their feeling level. Yes, they walk and talk with confidence, but under that facade they are frightened and lonely. When men act in an egotistical way they are simply revealing their insecurities. I believe that men long to connect, to love, and to be loved because that is a natural human need.

I am concerned that perhaps some women today who have reached great heights in their careers may feel superior to men and not act compassionately toward the men in their lives. Let's remember that personal achievement doesn't come from what we do; it comes from who we are! We are women empowered to bring love and wisdom into the world. I know this seems tough to handle. Well, we take a step at a time and do the best we can. There are many women who first need to concemtrate on the basics of loving themselves before they can help their man in any way.

I consider this an extremely challenging time for women because the natural order of things will insist on balance at some point. We will all need to look at our day-to-day activities to see what is pulling us away from finding true meaning in our lives. I am speaking of what woman really is all about. She is the nurturing force of life, but she is so much more. Woman is capable of doing almost anything, but she needs to be in touch with her inner wisdom so she does not squander her talents and her reason for being here. She needs to believe in herself and express who she is.

And where the children are concerned, women know what to do. Motherly wisdom flows through us naturally. We are the spiritual teachers. We teach others by working on elevating our own lives so that we are examples of love, protection, and understanding. I know some of you are not ready to accept this huge calling, and that is okay. It is a tall order, and I agree that it doesn't seem fair. But that's the way it is! Many times, it has been my inclination to say, "Why do we have to do it all?" Yes, I struggle with it myself.

Through writing this book, I have had so many new insights that have caused me to get down on my knees and give thanks for where I am in my life and for the new experiences that have opened up for me. So, if I am tempted even to think I must change my husband, or anyone else, I remind myself that my job is to lovingly help others discover their own strengths, at their own time. It also is my job to grow in greater awareness of who I am and what I am called to do. And, above all, it is my job to love in a way that I have not known before. It's like looking through a new lens and seeing the great possibilities ahead of me.

This does not require me necessarily to take on more responsibility. Somewhere along the line I, and many other women, have felt responsible for too much. I completely agree with women who ask their partners for more help with domestic duties. Men rarely understand what is involved in running a household. We women desperately need men who will cheerfully and lovingly assist us. As we travel our pathway of freedom of choice in how we express our talents, we need help with the many responsibilities we have already taken on. With more women focusing on themselves, the men are having to adjust to the new rules. Maybe we need to talk with our partners and lovingly tell them how we feel and ask them to have patience as we make our own transformation.

One thing I have learned is that we must trust our ability to let go of some of the preconceived notions about men and begin to see them with new eyes, thus changing the energy we give out from negative to positive. I know this may sound like a lot, but there is much at stake right now. Marriages are crumbling beneath distrust, misunderstandings, and the unwillingness of partners to seek help. Why do we resist our own growth? All the signs are here to tell us to try to understand our differences rather than continue blaming each other for how we think and how we feel.

I want to focus on this idea of men and women being different. What are those differences? And, do we ever stop and think about that when we are in a hot discussion with our partner or brooding over his inability to see things as we do? A very delightful and insightful book on that subject is *Men Are From Mars, Women Are From Venus*. I'm sure many of you have read it, but did you put some of the ideas into action? The author, John Gray, spells out how differences in communicating emotional needs and modes of behavior can promote greater understanding between partners.

John spent seven years researching ways to help develop and refine the insights about men and women. I have read this book with great interest and amazement at how the differences John came up with rang so true for me. We struggle so in our relationships, but I believe we need to educate ourselves on men and women's differences first, and then proceed in working with our partners to heal the wounds that have been inflicted.

We need to learn to relate with, listen to, and support the opposite sex. Understanding the differences can help to resolve a lot of frustration in day-to-day living with our partner. As we become open to looking at the men in a new way, we can learn to forgive and have increased motivation for creating a more loving partnership. It seems to me we try all kinds of quick fixes, but until we get down to the nitty-gritty of where the problems originate, we continue to be angry and frustrated.

I urge every one of you to purchase John Gray's book and begin to use some of the very wise ideas to help revitalize your partnership and relieve yourself of many of your irritations. I am not saying this book has all the answers to your problems, but I think it has ideas of great value in bringing men and women to a place where they can better accept each other. There is so much more that can get in the way of having a healthy relationship. One or both partners may be experiencing addictions, unresolved anger, stubbornness, and a need to be right. Let's be honest about looking at our own lives and move out in love as we work toward reaching the men in a new way.

We have made immense progress regarding the rights of women, but it appears we are at a crucial point where we have to look at how our lives are right now and decide on what direction we plan to go. We can take a path that leads to the total breakdown of relationships between the sexes, or we can take the path that leads to love. I believe that deep within our hearts we all have the human need to love and to be loved. So, the step that seems logical now is to set aside our hurt feelings, insecurities, fears, and expectations, which certainly applies to men as well, and find some common ground to work through our differences.

I know women want to be the best of who they are. In order for this to happen, we must access that place within that is creative, caring, truthful, confident, and loving. Looking for a man who will "take care of us" won't work in our new approach to marriage. That's focusing on me-me-me. When love is selfish, it does not seek to protect and nourish.

I stand behind what I have written earlier about a woman being fulfilled. It's just that some of us have to first clean up our act a bit. We may not be able to have it all right now. We, as women, have won many battles and have had many gains in changing perceptions and feelings, especially in the area of realizing our career goals. A multitude of new opportunities exist for women today, and these opportunities are increasing as both women and supportive men continue to deal with the inequalities that remain. While healthy relationships were difficult prior to the women's movement, for too many of us, they seem impossible today. With all of the gains we have made at this point in time, what has gone astray ? It is good to be independent and to have found at least part of who we are, but until we find the proper balance in our day-to-day living, we will continue to blame men.

Men are going through major changes at this time as many women choose to work outside of the home for their own self-worth and self-fulfillment. I believe we, as women, must use compassion as we continue to strive for that which fulfills us and remember that men *do* have insecurities. Continually venting frustration and anger won't change anything in a positive way.

Yes, it is very difficult for us to be patient with men who can't understand why we feel the way we do. Well, they haven't been where we have, and we haven't been where they have. Yes, if they could walk in our shoes for a month they would see more clearly our frustrations. And if we could walk in their shoes for a month we would have more patience. Some husbands *do* take on some of the household duties when the wife works, and that is only fair. But when there is a reluctance by a husband to do this we must understand all of the early conditioning that has gone before that says it is not their job. We need to exercise patience as we continue to move forward in our quest to help heal our relationships.

Changes are coming. Meanwhile, communicate with your man, and let him know what you are doing. Discuss the differences between the sexes with him that may bring about some change in attitudes and in accepting certain household responsibilities. You may have bottled up a lot of resentment for a long time, and you just want to get out of the marriage. But that is not the way to create a healthy understanding of what is required in forming a good relationship.

I believe men really want to know a woman's deepest

self. They can be good listeners, and we don't need to have a lot of feedback from them. When we learn more about "who we are," we are very capable of sharing it with our women friends, but let us also include our partners. I know certain problems in relationships present themselves because we really don't know how the other person feels. We are all trying to learn new skills in communicating. Learn something from the relationship you are in. And, if you see you cannot weave into it mutual understanding, trust, and the willingness of both parties to sincerely give their all in saving the relationship, move on.

Let's face it, we want to have it all, but we need to be patient in working through the various issues that have caused so much of the friction in our love relationships. There is already a consciousness in our present society that thinks more is better. Spending more money to satisfy this belief has become part of the problem between men and women, and God knows what it has done to our children. Even if both spouses agree on how they spend the money, there is frustration and anger over accumulating big debts. This makes it mandatory for many women to work whether they choose to or not.

I believe that women need to have the feeling of earning a good salary, but not to use it as a power tool. Being financially independent can offer women a lot, but if it also breaks up the family, it becomes a crisis. I feel this is a time for all of us to look at our own lives and to see where our values lie. We need to cooperate with each other to help balance out our lives, to see what is most important to us, individually and collectively. Having money gives us a certain amount of freedom, and that is good, but money will not buy a loving marriage, and it will not mend a broken heart.

We, as women, have made tremendous strides in finding our right place in society. Stories abound regarding how women have become financially independent. We are finally being respected for the various positions in business we hold, and the number of women senators are growing to the point where it is now realistic that some day we could have a woman president. All of this is wonderful, but how are our relationships working?

I have seen tendencies in myself where the ego rises up to claim its power through some rather unloving remarks that are said in jest, yet can be hurtful. We do not need to get "puffed up" over our achievements. I know it has been a long wait for some of us to rise up and express our talents. But, let's use our wonderful feminine qualities to assist us in respecting and helping the men in our lives while also serving our own self-growth. I certainly agree that men also need to change, and somewhere within each woman is the awareness of how to introduce to those men, who have not already learned it, that we want cooperation, we want inclusion and we want appreciation. And, we are apt to get it if we, first, cooperate and open our hearts to them.

I have looked at my own life, and I see how much I have to work on the things I am sharing with you. We all need to strive toward mending the errors of the past. Let's stop hiding behind our fears and our frustrations. Let's all join in to heal the separation that often happens between men and women.

I really don't think we need to give up that which we have struggled for. I believe if we are living out of who we really are, we can only gain a better sense of self and increase our capacity to love and be loved. For myself, I see a need to better understand the qualities of men and the way they think. I have come to believe if we honor their qualities and their needs without feeling we have to step in and change them, we can bring about the cooperation that we, as women, need.

And I think it is fair to say most women have some of the masculine qualities. And yes, I think it is possible some of us have not been willing to accept, as our own, certain masculine traits such as aggressive, arrogant, egotistical, and sometimes hostile behavior. It is going to take a lot of love and understanding to work toward coming together with men and realizing they are not the enemy. We, as women, must take responsibility for who we are, and that includes whatever masculine traits we have. And it will become necessary for men to accept some of their feminine qualities, such as nurturing, compassion, and receptivity. It's a matter of claiming who we are right now and moving toward healing those parts of ourselves that keep us from having the love we desire. We're all in need of looking deeper within ourselves to recognize certain disowned behavior that can fracture a relationship. Isn't it love, acceptance, and understanding we all want?

I think we women have been doing the best we could with the understanding we have had, but it is time to take the spiritual challenge and grow in all aspects of our lives. Both men and women are getting in touch with their pain, and it is challenging working through it to bring about the love and acceptance we so dearly want and need.

I don't know about you, but I know that I want to work toward this end. I am willing to take responsibility for many aspects of my relationship with my husband in a way that will heal any hurts that rise up. I love myself enough to work on these issues. Until men and women grow in their own self-worth and self-love, we will continue to hurt ourselves and hurt each other. Be willing to open your heart to being all you are meant to be. Be aware that men will feel very vulnerable as they see you change, and it will take great courage on their part to participate in their own journey to wholeness. Recognize they may have great confusion over making changes, and they may hold within them deep hurts that will require from us greater patience and understanding.

I feel we, as women, are ready to take on this task, not reluctantly, but because we are capable of turning things around in our relationships and creating more love and understanding.

CHAPTER NINE
AGING GRACEFULLY

Do you notice how much is being written and talked about today concerning aging? It is not too difficult to figure out that we are putting on a new mind-set concerning what older people are capable of doing. My studies and my own inner wisdom tell me to grasp onto this stage of life because it can offer me a quality of life that surpasses what older people have formerly believed to be possible. I am learning that we can age with grace and wisdom, and we can age with energy and vitality to handle our day-to-day experiences. That doesn't mean we will have the energy of young women.

For myself, simplifying my life has helped immensely. I am much kinder with myself, weighing the importance of the tasks that sometimes have me rushing too much. I give myself a lot of the simple pleasures like going for a walk, admiring my garden, reading a good book, watching a treasured movie from the past, or just sitting and contemplating. When I am tired, I rest. I'm introspective by nature, so I tend toward more quiet moments. Your simple things may be different.

Aging can mean accepting short-term memory loss, diminished vision or hearing, and less stamina as inevitable parts of growing older. It makes sense that we do some slowing down.

Personally, I wouldn't want that same youthful energy. We are where we are in our lives because nature is simply doing what she does, and it is perfect!

Allow yourself to go through the periods of uncertainty and even what may appear to be a sense of losing some of your faculties. You probably don't forget as much as you think. Most of it is fear of losing control, and yet, isn't it easier not to control everything. . . to just flow with it? Be very kind and gentle with yourself. I have found this to be the key in moving forward in my own life. It is never too late to learn this. We will be with ourselves up to the end, so be your own best friend. Nurture yourself, do the things that make you feel good, and forgive yourself for not always doing something the way you used to.

We definitely need to cooperate with the process of aging. I find that having somewhat of an agenda helps, and I consciously remind myself to work at these ideas. Some of you may have physical limitations, and they need to be taken into consideration. But, it doesn't mean you cannot live a full life. It just means it will be different! We'll probably live longer than we think, so we need to cultivate a healthy mind and begin to look seriously at how we can better take care of our bodies. The goal is to improve the quality of our senior years, not necessarily to prolong life. But, it is likely it also will extend our lifetime, depending on whether or not disease has already made itself known, how we care for our bodies right now and, of course, the genetic influences. My own agenda includes:

— Gracefully accepting the aging process
— Nurturing myself
— Strengthening my mind through mental activity

— Strengthening my muscles through simple exercises
— Improving my personal relationships
— Simplifying my life and doing things I really enjoy
— Getting adequate rest
— Forgiving others and forgiving myself
— Gently touching myself
— Prayer and meditation

We are all different, so you need to find what is important to you. Note, I have not included nutrition in my agenda. There is so much written on this subject and much of it is confusing and contradicting. I feel if you learn to really love and honor yourself, you will also seek out a nutritional program which is right for you. This becomes automatic once you have made a commitment to becoming a whole person.

Aging is inevitable. It is part of the life cycle in which the hair grays, the skin becomes less elastic, the eyesight a bit foggy, the reflexes slower, and the risk of disease may become greater. So, can we at least accept this much about the aging process? Many have gone before us proving that age did not prevent them from attaining great accomplishments. We don't have to be a Picasso, Grandma Moses, or Michelangelo. It would be enough to recapture some of our own dreams.

If you always wanted to draw or paint, begin with simple sketching or painting and see where it goes. Or, start a collection, learn to dance, or do some writing. Remember, the goal is to enjoy what you are doing. One of my very early dreams was to take flying lessons, but as the years have passed I think I'll have to pass on that one. My later dream of writing a book has become a reality. Let's not allow all of our dreams to fade away unaccomplished. The creative process remains with us at all ages, so keep your mind active so you can create something that will bring true meaning to your life.

How many of your dreams got lost along the way? How can you come to terms with the way your life is now, even with the broken dreams, health challenges, and certain losses in your life? I believe the mind is powerful enough and the spirit most willing to create a new way of thinking that will allow us to take some new form of action in our lives. The potential of the human spirit is clearly long lasting, so as we soften a bit in later life and open up to the treasures within us, a better life is assured us. I don't mean that we will totally change ourselves, nor should we, but we can put some of the demons we have created in our minds to rest. And, we can create some of the dreams we once had or create those we never had, but in a way that works for us now in our later years. Life is for living, not merely existing.

I have been writing about opening up our hearts. We don't want to carry resentment and ill will into our later years. If you are holding on to old wounds, put your hand on your heart and ask it to give you a new perspective on why you still need those feelings. As long as we criticize, blame, and withhold our love from others, we cannot hope to bring the joy and peace into our own lives. A closed heart can bring you only pain and suffering. Oh, it may not be a physical pain, but it will be an inner pain that prevents love from finding you. Let go of your fears and resentments and enter into these later years with a new perspective on life.

Know there is a part of you that can forever be young. I know this is true because most of the time I do feel young in so many ways. Sometimes I look in the mirror and wonder who this person is staring back at me. There is a part of me that feels much younger than the reflection in the mirror. I found this poem some time ago and it held a great deal of meaning for me:

STAYING YOUNG

The Spirit never ages.
The essence of the soul
Is sure and strong forever,
And keeps us young and whole.

The body shows that time has passed
When lines enrich the face,
When sight and hearing weaken,
When movement lacks in grace.

And, yet we know that deep within,
We're winsome, bright and fair,
Just as we were when we were young
And life was ours to dare!
    —Charlotte Pease

Something within us is alive, wanting to participate in life. Let us not limit our thinking and our actions only to that which appears to be so. We are much more than the physical, and we are much more than the intellect. We are spirit. We are of that stuff that is creative and eternal. Spirit knows what we need. Whatever our fears have created we can change, and a new creation can come forth as we let go of our destructive thinking habits. It doesn't matter how old we are or how physically ill we are. It doesn't matter that right now we feel unloved and useless.

We can start where we are this very moment. What matters now is that we hold on to that part of us that is alive and screaming for our recognition of it. That is spirit. It does not require us to be religious, but only willing to free ourselves of the broken dreams and the belief that we are a victim of life. There is a sustaining power in the universe that can help us to find hope again and to feel that life is worth living.

The human spirit is fragile. Treat yourself lovingly. Be willing to forgive yourself. Let life really touch you! Take care of unfinished business, especially involving unresolved love. Open your heart to those who seemingly have hurt you in some way. The past cannot be changed, but we can change the present. As we diligently change our attitudes and perceptions, we begin to create a different reality for ourselves. That new reality supports the belief that we have something to offer life, and that life has incredible experiences in store for us that will make living worthwhile. With every sad moment you have, life simultaneously is beckoning you to take its hand and walk together through the difficult times, having faith that something new is in process--a new creation!

Medical science is constantly making advances in ways to physically heal the human species, but as yet, most doctors do not speak with patients about how the human spirit can heal. However, there are the select few who have bravely crossed the line and will never again deal with their patients strictly on scientific terms. There are more and more complaints from patients who are adversely affected by medications to the point where they are willing to go beyond what medical science can do.

In addition to the new interest in alternative methods of healing, it is apparent to me we will still have to go even deeper; to look inside of ourselves for the answers. When I use the term healing I am referring to mind, body, spirit, and emotions. I believe when we give ourselves "quiet time" to go within and connect with our Divine source, healing will take place. It may not always be as you imagined it or wanted it, but there will be a healing. In my own life I have recognized that I must begin by healing attitudes and beliefs before the body will respond with more vibrant health. You may want to ask yourself the following questions:

— What beliefs do I need to let go of?
— What fears and resentments can I release?
— What parts of my body are crying out to me?
— Can I refrain from judging and controlling other people?
— What is my heart telling me about forgiveness?
— What is my heart telling me about my relationships?
— Am I willing to release my wounds from the past?

It's time to let go of all our old baggage. It's just too heavy to carry around. Let it go and make room for true love to enter. There is more to life if you will open your heart and let it guide you.

One of the changes women go through as we age is menopause, or change of life. This stage of life is part of who we are, and it is an important time for us. But, we have been taught that this is a time of our life we must dread. It is time to change that belief. Fortunately, prior to having menopausal symptoms I was introduced to ideas that made a huge difference in how I viewed this change of life. I was told this time is a rite of passage into the wisdom years. Now, I realize this will be a tough one to swallow if you have suffered through menopause with hot flashes, sleepless nights, and what is known as the "hormone blues." You may have thought you went through a rite of passage to hell!

But, we can change our perceptions and attitudes of what it means to go through this natural cycle of our life. There is so much we need to learn about our bodies during the aging process. Chronic stress adversely affects us because it drains the adrenal glands that have come in to help us at a time when our estrogen level drops. Seek out ways to release the stress in your life. Also, it is important we help ourselves by staying on a good, nutritional diet. Junk food does not nourish us.

There is so much I do not know yet, but new information comes when we begin to take charge of our bodies. We are alerted to many things that we can do for ourselves that help to create new vitality. It may come through some total stranger, through a book someone recommended, or through a holistic doctor. You can give yourself a truly wonderful gift by being open to new ways of healing the mind, body, spirit, and emotions. This is an act of loving yourself.

Even in our so-called advanced age of technology, the experience of aging is very outdated. Now is the time for women to get their own mind-sets changed in order to write a new definition of a woman's life after fifty. Dr. Christiane Northrup expounds on this in her book, *Women's Bodies, Women's Wisdom*. I ask women everywhere not to buy into the nonsense that we will all lose our femininity, and that our bodies will shrivel up in our post-menopausal years. This is ridiculous. There is help out today that can guide us in a new way to meet our later years.

It is true that the body often is subject to disease as we age, but part of that is due to not always taking good care of ourselves physically, emotionally, and spiritually. It is crucial that we begin to see that menopause is a natural process, and that we can begin to find ways to help ourselves through this precious and meaningful time of a woman's life. We must let go of the mentality that somehow has crept into the minds of women that we are not of much use when we reach menopause. We need to counteract such thinking because it simply is not true.

Menopause is not a mistake of Mother Nature. Women in other cultures appear to make the transition without so many problems and many glide through it with great ease. But, if you are among the many women who have suffered through menopausal changes, you may be helped by what I am sharing.

By the time we reach menopause most women have spent a good deal of our lives in childbearing and child rearing. If a woman has not had a satisfying job or career outside of the home, there is still time to find something meaningful in her life that brings fulfillment into each day. It may take learning entirely new ways of thinking about who she is.

Tamara Slayton in her book, *Reclaiming the Menstrual Matrix*, writes,

> "The natural expression of personal power and wisdom
> available to women during menopause is thwarted and
> frustrated in our culture. This surge of energy is subse -
> quently turned inward on oneself and can result in many
> unpleasant symptoms such as hot flashes, depression,
> mood swings, and a general feeling of being lost and
> unable to find a new and vital identity."

We are not lost; we merely need to change our thinking and attitude about aging. As we look around us, we see many women in their fifties and sixties who hold high positions in business and in public office. Many women begin to write very late in life. And there are an endless number of other things that older women are doing today that was unheard of thirty or forty years ago. Some women love having more time to create something new with their homes and gardens. If this gives them pleasure and satisfaction, it can be a wonderful way to express creativity. It really is up to us to find fulfillment in our lives.

It is evident that women are making progress in establishing new rules that can better guide us in our later years, and society is going along with them. We are even seeing more new jobs being created for seniors in the workplace.

I feel there is so much more that needs to be learned and revealed about how and why certain women's bodies go through drastic changes at different times of their lives. I can only touch on a small portion of information in this book. However, I have suggested certain reading on the last page of my book that will help educate you. We, as women, need to know we are not victims! Menopause is a natural state of our development and is a *beneficial part of our journey*.

Certainly, we deserve to be given the very best advice available in the prevention of certain menopausal problems, but it seems to me many doctors simply prescribe estrogen without even considering possible alternatives. I suggest you get the book, *What Your Doctor May Not Tell You About Menopause*, by John Lee, M.D. I have used this book as a reference for many things concerning my body. Dr. Lee includes a wealth of information far beyond that which concerns menopause. His focus has been on assisting women to be all they are meant to be. This book will help you learn what questions to ask your doctor.

If we can remind ourselves that menopause is the beginning of the second half of life, we will be more inclined to make some plans for enriching our lives. Get in touch with those feelings you have stuffed because you felt it wouldn't do any good to hope for anything better. Those feelings are important because they will help you to see they have something to do with your true purpose in life.

It is important that we recognize that the process of change is never easy. And aging is one of the bigger changes in life. Many fears come up, and one of the greatest fears of growing older seems to be "Will I become senile?" Statistics show that the percentage of older people who become senile is very small, but we need to keep our minds active so our chances of losing a sharpness of mind is limited. And we need to eat nutritional food. Stress affects our ability to think clearly. If you feel stressful on a regular basis get help. Prayer helps. Meditation helps. Calling a loved one may help. Using a relaxation technique is good. Releasing your pent-up feelings allows new energy to come in. Understanding what is stressing you helps because you can set out to change a situation if only in your perception or attitude about it. Stressful living situations keep us from using all of our mental capabilities.

It is good to quiet our minds, letting the constant inner chatter go. Clearing the busy mind through "quiet time" can do wonders. It helps us to touch our inner source of wisdom. Quiet time, prayer, and meditation are all extremely helpful in accessing that part of you that can bring you new hope and a feeling of being safe. Have you ever noticed when someone is praying, whether at home or at church, you are feeling calm and safe? You aren't feeling fear at this time. Holding on to our fears creates stress. I remember both my mother and grandmother praying and reading the Bible. They knew how to find solace in the Divine.

Remember, you are in charge of your life now. What are you going to do to comfort yourself when you are stressed out? I have tried to give you enough ideas so that you will find your journey much easier. Take time to contemplate some of this material. Be still and ask your inner wisdom whether or not these ideas make sense to you. Underline parts of the book so you can easily go back to reread certain information. Check out the Suggested Reading list in the back of the book. By all means, stay with your agenda.

Especially as we age, we need to establish some new habits. This is a challenge because often we have a tendency to hold on to old belief patterns that no longer serve us well. As we reach our sixties and seventies, we usually can find time to do the things that nourish us and fulfill us. However, our old habits often keep us from moving in a new direction. I'm not suggesting you change everything, but limited thinking keeps us from using the creative energy we have. The concentration it takes to form a new habit is very good exercise for your brain.

Loneliness is an issue with many older people, and it can be frightening especially if you live alone. It is sad to think that many people feel lonely even while living with someone else. If you are looking for someone else to make life better for you, you just may be stuck with your loneliness. That feeling of emptiness within can make you think there is no way you can feel full again. Don't buy into this. Something within you knows how to feel full. Especially as we age, we need to keep our minds active and open ourselves to new ways in which we can find meaning in our lives. I realize this is not a simple thing to do.

If you constantly feel lonely, get some help, and hold tight to your faith in a greater power. I lived alone for nineteen years before I remarried, and I felt some loneliness from time to time. I found if I would begin to write about the way I was feeling and begin to dip into the well of knowledge that I had, I would stimulate myself enough to think differently. Also, I have come to think that sometimes we have to feel lonely in order to get in touch with a deeper part of ourselves that has been pushed down for so long. Perhaps we have numbed ourselves so we can no longer feel the pain of some particular event and it needs to be brought to the surface for healing.

Through my many challenges in life, I don't think I could have survived without feeling the Divine Presence within me. I remember several times when fear entered and the Twenty-Third Psalm from the Bible immediately came to me. The passage that helped most was, "Ye though I walk through the valley of the shadow of death, I will fear no evil, for thou art with me. Thy rod and thy staff they comfort me." I would imagine myself actually walking *through* the challenge being comforted and guided by my Divine source. It takes a good deal of courage and faith to walk through the difficult times. Remind yourself that you are never alone. Your greater power is always available to you. But, also, get some help from human beings who are warm and loving. Understanding friends or family can also still your fears and you can begin to see that your needs will be met.

A PRAYER

Help me to let go of my fears.

I am ready to open up to new ways of thinking.
I ask for Divine guidance.
I quiet myself right now and listen to my inner voice.
I give thanks for this new attitude I have.
I am willing to walk the journey to wholeness.

As we age, there is a great need to be touched. In that regard, we become as an infant again. I ask the younger people who read this book to be with the elders in your life. The human touch says we are cared for and we are loved. Please don't wait until your loved ones are ill before you touch them. Communicate this way to the older people in your life. Just putting your hand on one cheek, or taking their hand and holding it, can lift their spirits. If you are older and live alone seek out ways you can have human contact, but also touch yourself.

Do not hesitate to ask for help. Ask your doctor regarding sources of contact or find out about activities that are going on in your local senior center. Talk to a minister. Their love and compassion can help you. I, personally, don't think having people around us all the time is necessarily the answer, but we are all different. Every situation is unique. As with any other time in our lives, a healthy attitude helps us to get through the difficult times.

Try to get over the nonsense that aging is bad. If you have a serious health problem, I realize the later years can be much more challenging. However, I have met many people with debilitating health problems, yet their attitude was uplifting. Some have made me wonder if I could handle such a situation as well. In any event, aging is inevitable, and it is a natural process. But, we have not yet come to understand that our later years can bring us greater peace, understanding, and wisdom.

Certainly, we have something to offer those who follow us and that is experience and the understanding that a greater power is always with us. We have more time to devote to spiritual studies. . . more time to devote to family and friends. . . and more time to go within and tap our inner wisdom. So, we need never be alone. There are so many ways we can help ourselves if we come from a place of really wanting to live.

I can tell when I am talking with someone who has already made up her mind that she is not ready to change. I hear a lot of negativity, little or no planning for the future, and there is a total complacency about her. There is nothing wrong with this if someone chooses to stay the way they are. We have to honor their free choice. I think it is also important to consider that some older women who appear to give up are actually turning their attention inward, feeling they have fulfilled their task of becoming the person they were born to be. This particular woman needs to turn her natural receptivity toward the inner whisperings of her soul.

We cannot always reason from the basis of the human mind, especially when we are experiencing a challenge. But, allowing something greater than ourselves to instill in us the wisdom beyond what we could possibly even imagine, the fears lessen, and we are assured of moving through the experience better equipped to handle it. No, it is not easy to do this. On my own pathway to healing I have had many challenges in letting go and allowing my Divine source to direct me.

The one that brought me the most emotional pain was concerning my daughter who struggled with alcoholism for about fourteen years. At first, I was uneducated about this disease, and I was devastated to think this was happening to my daughter and to our whole family. She was in many recovery places, but her obsession with alcohol continued. I read everything I could get my hands on hoping it would help me. I prayed that answers would come to her, and I cried a lot. I was told by Al-Anon groups that I must let go. . . that I must not enable my daughter.

The years that followed brought me even greater emotional pain. I prayed for strength and guidance. My daughter was so close to self-destruction that it was frightening. Here was my child I carried in my womb, brought into this world, and nurtured with my love. I knew part of me could not totally let go. I held the image in my mind of her free of this terrible disease. While I kept in touch with her by mail, I rarely saw her during her active drinking. It was too painful and it could have led to a dependency that would only have enabled her. This was the most difficult thing I have ever had to do.

But, it taught me a lot about accepting things that I could not change. I struggled with what might be appropriate for her. She is sober today, active in AA and committed to her spiritual journey. I enjoy her so much, and we have an extremely close relationship. The pain endured through those years has allowed me great joy now, but I certainly didn't understand that while I was caught up in fear and feeling I must come up with the answer to create sobriety for her. It is at these most difficult times that we need the spiritual guidance to help us discern what is appropriate and what is not. During the process of soul searching I received insight and understanding beyond what I could possibly have comprehended earlier.

I am convinced that once we move through the greatest challenges, hanging tight to our faith, we will be able to handle all of life's challenges quite well. In the very difficult emotional situations, we all fall short of letting go. After all, we are human. Letting go allows us to loosen up physically. Under stress our bodies tense up and we are easily thrown off balance. I have had to learn that I cannot play God. I do what I can do, and I turn it over to the loving universe to handle. I think I am finally getting it! We all have a reluctance toward letting go. Sometimes we hang on as though our very life is at stake, but the stress of it takes its toll.

Letting go is a process. You have to know when to apply it, what to let go of, and how to let go. Your mind is not going to show you any of these things since it believes that you have to hold on in order to survive. Your only ally in letting go is spirit, which sees reality in a different way. The process of letting go must be taken in small steps. By being willing to change and to carve out a few minutes each day to be still and ask for Divine guidance and direction, we discover that new awareness comes in. This new awareness is what helps us to see things from a different perspective.

I believe learning to let go is extremely important, especially as we age. Some of us have been carrying too much unnecessary baggage for so long that we feel loaded down. We are concerned over our children, our grandchildren, our spouse, and lots of other people in our lives, not to mention our own health and financial security. I know many of you have been hurt deeply, and you may need to return once again to weep the tears which are still unshed. Free yourself by coming to a greater understanding of what life wants from you. Let the tears come and let them wash away your pain. Begin to forgive others, and please forgive yourself.

We need to break the chains of bondage on ourselves. This is a clue that we need to let go and allow something greater than ourselves to resolve the issues at hand. Part of letting go is releasing the need to control. We need to get rid of the anger, resentment, and wanting to run the show. This is the time in our lives where we really need to be in touch with our intuition that can guide us in so many ways to take proper action at the proper time. And, please don't give up those dreams that still have a seed of possibility in them.

Some time ago I bought a book that has touched the hearts of millions of people because it tells a beautiful story about living. The book is *Tuesdays with Morrie*, which has been on the best-seller list since 1996. It is the story of a college professor who touched many lives during his tenure by speaking about the important things in life, as he saw them. He spoke of being authentic; of seeking out the true meaning of life. The story is centered around the visits of a former student who ended up writing the book as the professor was dying.

Because of the many friends Morrie made over the years, he had an incredible number of visitors, and it was an opportunity for him to further share his thoughts about life and death from an even greater perspective. He spoke of the times of disappointment and heartbreak, but always feeling there is a reason for everything, and that we need to learn to trust that good will come from it. I highly recommend this book to everyone, but especially to those who are reaching older age. Your hearts will be touched, and I know you will gain wisdom and feelings of assurance for yourself that you can create a life you once thought impossible.

As an older woman myself, I know I have shed a lot of

meaningless things and negative preoccupations. I hope I have become softer, more gentle, and more understanding. I know so much more about who I am right now. I can be more compassionate with myself by not judging myself for doing things earlier in my life that I now recognize as unloving. If we can accomplish this much as aging women, we can be sure that we have been chosen to show the younger women how they can grow old gracefully.

You younger women can begin now to prepare yourselves for the later years by focusing on your spiritual strength so by the time you have matured and reached your peak of blossoming, you will leave a beautiful legacy for your children, grandchildren, and all who share your presence. Growing old can be a blessing if we will continue to search our hearts for what our creator wants from us. It doesn't have to mean a busyness, but rather an energy that can reach others in ways we do not even understand. Being in my later years, I can give much more of my love and devotion to my loved ones and to those I meet than I could in my early years.

Give serious thought to what you would like to do during the later years of life. Life calls to you at every age, so be ready to answer the call. Many older women say, "Is this all there is?" Those who feel this way have not tuned in to their inner wisdom. It's time to release the fears and go deeper within yourself to see what life is calling you to do. Allow your creativity to come through. It could be your last chance to do what you have always wanted to do. It doesn't have to be a major project. This is not about satisfying the ego. It's about glorifying the soul.

CHAPTER TEN

LIVING IN THE PRESENT

After we have wrestled with our past, it is good to put it aside. Yes, we will go back to it at times to clean out a little more. . . to appreciate more. . . to forgive more. . . to understand more. . . and of course to remind ourselves of the blessings along the way. But, it is right *now* that we need to look at. What are we doing *now* to create a brighter future for ourselves and for those we love? It is time to forgive ourselves for what we perceive as mistakes of the past.

Don't use your energy to "rake yourself over the coals" for things you might have done differently or better. It's time to get on with living! Each of us has something special to offer life, and by using our talents we, ourselves, become the benefactors. I hope some of the things I have shared in this book will help you to create something worthy of who you are. It doesn't have to be something that will bring fame and fortune. It can be something of great simplicity that brings joy to you and to those who share your presence.

Accept what is yours now and give thanks for it. Being grateful for what you have now is the surest way of always having what you need. Begin to shed the thinking that more is better. That kind of thinking puts you in a state of lack and limitation because you continue to believe you don't have enough. Just because you are grateful for what you have now doesn't mean you will not have any more. It merely is living in the present having faith that you will be taken care of by a power greater than yourself by letting this power direct your creativity into channels that benefit you. If you cling to things and people in your life and feel that this is where your security is, you will be disappointed. Instead, realize your own potential and ask for guidance to move in the direction that will be for your highest and best good.

Money does not assure you of being secure. Certainly, we need money to function in this world, but be aware that you don't think money will make you happy. Your security comes from building a trust in yourself and your greater power to bring forth what you need. If your energies only go into that which increases your financial worth, you will be blind to the other creative endeavors that need to be expressed.

Above all, be true to yourself. It is important that we all peel off any falseness and pretense that covers up who we are at the core of us. We deserve to be our "authentic self." By recognizing the value of honesty and sincerity in our personal lives we shall enrich not only our own lives, but those of others as well. A successful life is not successful because the person had no obstacles to overcome. It is successful because she overcame whatever obstacles were presented to her.

No life is without obstacles or setbacks. It is how we face and overcome these obstacles that makes the difference in our lives. We cannot always eliminate an obstacle, but by facing it realistically, accepting it for what it is, and handling it with courage, we overcome the stumbling block and become stronger in the process. Accepting what happens, and working with it, is somewhat like the trees swaying in the strong winds. If they were not flexible they would break and fall apart. By being flexible ourselves we can accept the obstacle and still come out the winner.

I am still learning to trust myself even more, but that can happen only when I am relying on my Divine source to guide me in all of the choices I make. I remind myself that with the Divine all things are possible. If my heart is telling me something is good for me, I do not waste my time worrying how I will accomplish it. I have learned that the heart can lead me to miracles. I need only be still and allow my good to come forth in whatever form that is right for me. Yes, I will need to take action myself, but I will be shown how to do that.

I need to continue to practice the principles that I say I believe in. It's not like flicking on a light switch and we have light. It takes practice in living the principles so these things become a part of our belief system. It was difficult at first to trust this way, but through so many good results, I am finally ready to let go and allow my greater power take charge of all my affairs. Will I always feel comfortable with this? I don't know. All I know is when I do this, my life unfolds in wonderful ways.

All of life is such a mystery. Things sometimes aren't as they appear, and time and space have a different meaning in the spiritual. So, as we think we know what we want and who we are, suddenly something changes, and that is the process of evolving as we open to inspiration and new awareness. Most of us are not used to living our lives completely open for change. We have been taught that anything that we cannot experience with our five senses has no value. It takes discipline to live by spiritual rules. We have to be willing to set time aside to go within and seek direction in our lives.

As I can well attest to, those of us with strong wills will struggle. We want solid proof that what we are doing will work, but part of the beginning process is to reach out in faith. The good news is we can begin to get in touch with the spiritual by slowing down. It won't happen if we fill every moment of every day with frantic activity and work. Sometimes I wonder whether or not a lot of our rushing around isn't an avoidance of confronting who we are deep within ourselves. And, our minds are on fire with so much data that it is difficult to hear what the small voice within us is trying to say. There is a far better way to live. Take the journey to wholeness.

Accept that you have the power to do what you are meant to do. And, accept that you are wonderfully unique being just who you are. Stay on the pathway of learning to love yourself, and forgiving yourself for things you wish you hadn't done. Know you deserve a fulfilling and loving life, so begin living it right now. Don't wait until tomorrow or next week. Do it NOW!

Gain from your experiences by understanding everything has a purpose. Perhaps it is a time to see what needs cleaning up in your life. Break through your old beliefs and day-to-day living patterns so you can see clearly what you are doing for, or to, yourself. Now is also the time to release all the old wounds that have been brought to the surface. You no longer need to feed on them for sympathy or excuses for why your life is the way it is. They served their purpose, and now you can transform that pain into something worthwhile. You have the power to heal so much of your life if you can only refrain from thinking it is other people's actions that keep you from your good.

Go within to discover ways to change your life. Pull out

every single possibility of how you can change your perception and your attitude about what is happening in your life.

Quit looking for someone else to validate you, to make your life fulfilling, and to heal you of your emotional and physical challenges. Do you really think others have all the answers? Of course, you need people in your life to help point the way when you have found yourself out of balance and in need of help. But, can you come to a place where you realize you have the wisdom within yourself to heal so much in your life. Give up searching for the treasures outside of yourself; they are already within you. You just need to awaken to who you are and what you are assigned to do.

We go to doctors and health care practitioners for the answers.

We go to AA, Al-Anon, or other programs to get the answers to our frustrations and fears.

We go to our friends for advice.

We read the latest magazines on how to change ourselves.

And, finally, if all else fails, we go within and sincerely pray from our hearts to our Divine source regarding what we, ourselves, need to do to heal our lives.

Some of these sources can be extremely helpful, but first and foremost look within yourself for the answers that will bring healing in your life. Give yourself the love, peace, and joy that you so dearly seek. To do this you must give up your fears. Fears bring you a false illusion of what is happening in your life. Remember, you are in charge of your thoughts. Let them be thoughts that empower you to create your dreams.

During this writing, I have had to look at my own life and see whether or not I am living the kind of life that merits such a book. I can only say that from time to time I struggle with life issues just like anyone else. And, it is when I am faced with challenges that, again, I remind myself of what I say I believe. So, with every single challenge I turn into an opportunity, I add to my ability to trust myself. That is the key. We need to trust ourselves. Be willing to take charge of your life by trusting your "nudges" and by being willing to go through change.

While writing this book I have had to come to terms with things in my life that I did not even know were keeping me from greater peace and harmony. I am grateful that these things were made known to me so I can heal them. I continue to work on not becoming attached to specific results in my life for I know something within me guides me into what is right and good for me *now*. I know I cannot be complacent about where I am right now, for life itself has a way of awakening us to the new. There is so much that we just don't know about ourselves. . . our capacity to love, our yearnings to find peace, and our strength to embrace the unknown challenges of life. Do what you can do *now*, and life will support you along your journey.

It has been a wondrous adventure for me to put into words my deepest beliefs, the yearnings of my heart, and to share some of my life experiences with you. I hope some of the passages from this book will encourage you to listen to your own body and learn to trust its wisdom. I believe this is the only way we can go beyond the limited healing methods used today.

Remember, it isn't enough to use the intellect. Listen to what your heart is saying and bring it into alignment with your intellect. It is the heart that leads us to deeper understanding and awareness. Dare to say "yes" to your inner nudges, and please give yourself the gift of "quiet time."

Some of the ideas I have written about will be new to you. Take only that which belongs to you for now. I do not have the answers for creating a fulfilling, healthy, loving, and peaceful life for you. I give you ideas and possibilities. You create your own experience, and it will be in large part based on your belief system and your willingness to accept some of the unknown mysteries of life that reveal themselves through your deeper spiritual awareness.

I think it is important to understand that our beliefs go much deeper than our thoughts, and that we cannot just will them away. Many beliefs are subconscious, so in order to touch this part of our minds, we must rely on the spiritual process. This means having a relationship with the Divine where we ask to be given whatever will help us to create the life that brings greater meaning and purpose to us.

May each of you be blessed in a special way as you continue your journey to wholeness. Remember, it isn't your job to change the people in your lives. Your job is to awaken to your true self that has been asleep. Seek out the little girl within you and find out what she needs. Touch her, caress her, and let her know you are making changes that will help to heal her. I guarantee you there is so much more to you than you see at this time.

Life is about recognizing what real love is and to act out of that realization. Love isn't just a feeling. Love is a truth filled with forgiveness and kindness. It's a gift that is bursting with generosity and honesty. Love is the willingness to serve and protect, to cherish and respect, to honor and be strong. Look within yourself and discover these gifts yet to be accepted by you.

Don't be afraid to love, for it is in the love you give out, and the love you receive, that miracles come about. This includes loving yourself! Work toward bonding yourself with the people who enter your life and give them this new kind of love you have discovered. We can each make a difference in creating a world where it is truly safe to love each other.

We are women connected through our hearts, as well as our minds. Regardless of our religious beliefs, we are also connected spiritually. Regardless of our race, we join together as "one" in love. Let's put aside all judgments and criticisms and move toward honoring each other as we travel our *Journey to Wholeness*.

Commit now to living in a whole new way, a way that gives you permission to be who you really are. No one else can do it for you. Be kind and gentle with yourself as you travel your pathway to wholeness, and remember how very precious you are. Know that the next step to healing and living joyfully is already there waiting for you to discover it through your heart and to bring it into full expression. As you go within and listen to that small quiet voice, you will understand why you are here and what you are meant to do.

Suggested Reading

Anatomy of the Spirit, Caroline Myss, Ph.D.

Bradshaw on the Family, John Bradshaw

Healing the Child Within, Charles Whitfield, M.D.

Healing the Shame That Binds You, John Bradshaw

Legacy of the Heart, The Spiritual Advantages of a Painful Childhood, Wayne Muller

Men Are From Mars, Women Are From Venus, John Gray, Ph.D.

Minding The Body, Mending The Mind, Joan Borysenko, Ph.D.

Reclaiming the Menstrual Matrix, Tamara Slayton

Return to Love, Marianne Williamson

Sabbath, Restoring the Sacred Rhythm of Rest, Wayne Muller

Self-Parenting, John K. Pollard

The Power of Touch, Phyllis Davis

The Power of Your Subconscious Mind, Joseph Murphy, M.D.

The Road Less Traveled, M. Scott Peck, M.D.

The Road Less Traveled and Beyond, M. Scott Peck, M.D.

The Wisdom of Menopause, Christiane Northrup, M.D.

Tuesdays With Morrie, Mitch Albom

Wake-Up Calls, Gerald Jampolsky, M.D. & Diane Cirincione

What Your Doctor May Not Tell You About Menopause, John Lee, M.D.

What Your Doctor May Not Tell You About Breast Cancer, John Lee, M.D.

Why People Don't Heal and How They Can, Caroline Myss, Ph.D.

Women's Book of Confidence, Sue Patton Thoele

Women's Book of Spirit, Sue Patton Thoele

Women's Bodies, Women's Wisdom, Christiane Northrup, M.D.

You Can Heal Your Life, Louise L. Hay